Agriculture in India

Institutional Structure and Reforms

Agriculture in India

Institutional Structure and Reforms

By

Kartik Prasad Jena

Senior Reader, Department of Economics,
Bhadrak Autonomous College,
Fakir Mohan University,
Balasore, Odisha.

New Century Publications
New Delhi, India

NEW CENTURY PUBLICATIONS
4800/24, Bharat Ram Road,
Ansari Road, Daryaganj,
New Delhi - 110 002 (India)

Tel.: 011-2324 7798, 4358 7398, 6539 6605
Fax: 011-4101 7798
E-mail: indiatax@vsnl.com • info@newcenturypublications.com
www.newcenturypublications.com

Editorial office:
LG–7, Aakarshan Bhawan,
4754-57/23, Ansari Road, Daryaganj,
New Delhi - 110 002

Tel.: 011-4356 0919

First Published: **2014**

ISBN: **978-81-7708-380-4**

Published by New Century Publications and printed at Salasar Imaging Systems, New Delhi.

Designs: Patch Creative Unit, New Delhi.

PRINTED IN INDIA

This Book is Dedicated to My Father

Late Shri Narahari Jena

A Humble Farmer

Foreword

Economics of farm management during mid-1950s raised several important issues with respect to efficiency of small farms compared to large ones in terms of yield and value of output per acre.

What is the ideal size of a holding? The ideal size of a holding (called economic holding or optimum holding) is one which allows the most efficient use of land, labour and capital with a given technique of production. It is difficult to prescribe a uniform size of economic holding for all crops and for all regions. In fact, the size of economic holding depends upon a host of factors such as nature of the crop, fertility of soil and technique of production.

There is a great debate among agricultural economists in India regarding the relationship between size of farms and productivity/profitability. Productivity simply means output per hectare of land while farm-profitability relates to the value of output over all costs of cultivation. Some experts have argued that as farm size increases, productivity also increases. However, some researchers hold the opposite view and maintain that productivity declines as farm size increases. Although the debate is inconclusive and the picture confusing, it has been reasonably well established by statistical studies that farm size and productivity are inversely related. The myth that small farms are inefficient has been exploded. The opponents of land ceiling laws always criticised the break up of large farms on efficiency ground. Since the efficiency of small farms has nearly been confirmed, the case for land ceiling on equity ground has become stronger.

Agrarian structure is undoubtedly one of the most important determinants of farm efficiency. Therefore, it is believed that reorganization of agrarian structure is an essential and unavoidable necessity for agricultural development in an agrarian society like India, but its reorganization is a stupendous task. Agrarian structure does not merely relate to ownership of land, but in a broad sense, it includes the entire gamut of socio-economic structure of a pre-dominantly agrarian economy.

Dr. Kartik Prasad Jena has made concerted effort in his present work to explain and examine the institutional framework of Indian agriculture, and reforms thereof, in the areas of land reforms, agricultural credit, marketing of agricultural produce, and public distribution system (PDS).

The book is a timely contribution by the author. I am sure that this book would prove useful to policy makers, professionals, academicians and scholars.

Professor (Dr.) R.M. Mallik
Senior Fellow, I.C.S.S.R.
and Formerly Professor of Economics, N.C.D.S.
Bhubaneswar, Odisha

About the Book

Use of modern methods of production is conditioned by the institutional framework of a production sector. If the institutional set up is exploitative, it will discourage the adoption of efficient technology. Unfortunately, the institutional settings of the farm sector in India are not congenial for the use of modern agricultural techniques.

Although *zamindari* system was abolished soon after Independence in 1947, it continues to exist in a different garb. Land reform laws have proved ineffective and therefore big landlords still rule the roost in rural areas.

As a result of population growth, there is tremendous pressure on available cultivable land. This has led to overcrowding and hence sub-division and fragmentation of holdings. Small-sized and scattered holdings imply wastage of time and labour, difficulties in the use of modern techniques, and quarrels and litigation among farmers.

The institution of money lending is the greatest curse for the poor and illiterate rural folk of India. Although the importance of moneylenders has declined over the years, they are still very dominant in providing credit to the farmers. The exploitative practices of the moneylenders are no secret.

Furthermore, the present marketing system of agricultural produce is not favourable to the interests of the farmers. The preponderance of intermediaries and the malpractices of commission agents deny remunerative prices to the farmers.

This book explains and examines the institutional framework of Indian agriculture, and reforms thereof, pertaining to land management, land reforms, agricultural credit, marketing of agricultural produce, public procurement of agricultural produce and related areas.

Author's Profile

Dr. Kartik Prasad Jena is Senior Reader in Economics at Post-graduate Department of Economics, Bhadrak Autonomous College, Fakir Mohan University, Balasore, Odisha. He received M.A. and Ph.D. degrees from Utkal University. He is a distinguished life member of the Indian Economic Association (IEA), Indian Society of Agricultural Economics (ISAE), and Odisha Economics Association (OEA).

Dr. Jena successfully completed a research project on 'Consolidation of Land Holdings' funded by the University Grants Commission (UGC), New Delhi. He has published a number of research papers in professional journals of repute.

Contents

Preface

Indian agriculture was traditional and stagnant in every respect at the time of Independence in 1947. It was characterized by feudal land relations, primitive technology, and the resultant low productivity per hectare. The first task of Indian Government in the immediate post-Independence period was, therefore, to initiate growth process in agriculture on modern lines. Modernization of agriculture was required both in terms of technological and institutional changes. Abolition of intermediaries in agriculture, like *zamindars* and *jagirdars*, was accomplished soon after Independence.

Agricultural policy followed since Independence can be broadly classified into three phases. Phase one, immediately after independence, witnessed several institutional changes through land reforms and initiation of major irrigation projects. The second phase, since the mid-1960s, was aimed at increasing agricultural productivity to attain self-sufficiency in foodgrains through technological revolution and public support to credit, marketing, extension etc. This was followed by the current phase, since the late 1980s, aimed at making agriculture more market-oriented.

Use of modern methods of production is conditioned by the institutional framework of a production sector. If the institutional set up is exploitative, it will discourage the adoption of efficient technology. Unfortunately, the institutional setting of the farm sector in India is not congenial for the use of modern agricultural technology.

Although *zamindari* system was abolished soon after Independence, it continues to exist in a different garb. Land reform laws have proved ineffective and therefore big landlords still rule the roost in rural areas. They lease out their land to tenants and charge high rents. The various tenancy malpractices hardly provide any incentive to tenant farmers to improve land and productivity.

As a result of population growth, there is tremendous

pressure on available cultivable land. This has led to overcrowding and hence sub-division and fragmentation of holdings. Small-sized and scattered holdings imply wastage of time and labour, difficulties in the use of modern techniques, and quarrels and litigation among farmers. The existence of these problems is also responsible for poor farm yield.

Poverty of the Indian farmer forces him to borrow money for his existence. The institution of money lending is the greatest curse for the poor and illiterate rural folk of India. Although the importance of moneylenders has declined over the years, they are still very dominant in providing credit to the farmers. The exploitative practices of the moneylenders are no secret. Their malpractices include charging of high rate of interest and adopting unfair means in the maintenance of accounts.

Marketing is the last ring in the production chain. If the marketing system is inefficient and denies the farmers a reasonable return for their efforts, they will be discouraged to produce more. Unfortunately, the present marketing system of agricultural produce is not favourable to the interests of the farmers. The preponderance of intermediaries and the malpractices of commission agents deny remunerative prices to the farmers.

While agriculture no longer dominates the Indian economy in terms of national output, it is still the most important in terms of employment. In other words, declining share of income has not been accompanied by an equivalent decline in employment. It is a classic case of lop-sided structural transformation.

Accelerating the rate of growth of agricultural production is seen as central to a more inclusive growth.

While there have been efforts—such as those to promote institutional credit to rural areas, improved access to inputs, subsidies on fertilisers and electricity, minimum support price etc.—these have not been fully successful in protecting the interest of the farmers in general, and small/marginal farmers in particular. Small/marginal farmers have inadequate access to: (a) information, (b) agencies promoting technological change, (c) co-operative networks and related organisations, and (d) plethora of governmental interventions. This is significant since, in any case, these farmers are not well placed to take advantage of the markets.

Against the backdrop of the burgeoning demand of population for foodgrains, degrading natural resource base, emerging concerns of climate change and other challenges, the Government has focused on mobilizing higher investment in agriculture, bridging yield gaps that exist across the states/regions, timely and adequate supply of quality inputs, and providing adequate support services to the farmers to make agriculture a remunerative vocation on a sustainable basis. Increasing agricultural production with limited natural resources in a sustainable manner for ensuring food and nutritional security and providing income security to farmers are the major challenges before the Government.

Acknowledgments

I take this opportunity and privilege to record my deep sense of gratitude to Professor Radha Mohan Mallik, Senior Fellow of Indian Council of Social Science Research (ICSSR), New Delhi and the former Professor of Economics of Nabakrushna Choudhury Centre for Development Studies (NCDS), Bhubaneswar, for constantly encouraging me to complete this work and generously helping me with many valuable suggestions and critical comments.

Thanks are also due to my wife Sakuntala who has always been the source of my strength and without whose co-operation this work would not have seen the light of the day.

Bhubaneswar **Kartik Prasad Jena**

1

India's Land Resources: Problems and Management

India is endowed with many natural resources. However, land is the most important natural resource which is the base for agricultural, industrial and many other productive activities. With a total land area of 3,287,263 square kilometres, the country measures 3,214 kilometres from North to South and 2,993 kilometres from East to West. It has a land frontier of 15,200 kilometres and its sea coast runs to the length of 7,517 kilometres.

1.1 Pressure on Land Resources

After China, India is the most populous country in the world accounting for 17 percent of world population as per Census 2011. It is the seventh largest country in the world occupying 2.3 percent of total world area. It has 0.5 percent of the world's grazing area but has over 18.0 percent of world's cattle population. These pressures have led to drastic changes in the proportion of land utilised for agricultural activities, urbanisation and industrial development.

While population pressure grows, the land surface is fixed and only a certain proportion of it is available for cultivation. In the context of increasing human and animal population, the non-expandable land resources have to accommodate the competing demands for production of food, fodder, fibre, fuel, minerals, urbanisation, non-agricultural land use etc.

In the past, increase in net sown area came about by converting forest area into cultivable area. There is no such scope at present or in the near future. The only alternative available is to reclaim the waste land and the land suffering from salinity, alkalinity and water logging. In reclaiming available wasteland, private sector initiative and expertise should be tapped wherever necessary.

It is necessary to ascertain the extent to which land now lying waste can become available for cultivation. Increasing population also means withdrawal of areas now under farms for building houses. Development of communications such as roads, railways, and airways may take up fertile land. Owing to rapid urbanisation and growth of large cities land is needed for parks and open spaces. Irrigation dams may submerge fertile areas. Industrial plants and other establishments also require substantial areas. In the context of all these developments, wherever fertile land can be saved efforts should be made to do so. This indicates the need for a comprehensive inventory of land and for greater refinement in land classification and continuous attention to land use.

It is important to appreciate the inextricably close relationship between land and water management. Water, which is a renewable resource, can in fact be put to good use only if the land on which it falls, and the land to which it is applied, are properly cared for.

Land, which is for all purposes a non-renewable and inelastic resource, must be managed in such a manner as to be benefited rather than suffer damage as a result of its contact with water. The key to environmental quality, therefore, lies in scientific land and water management.

1.2 Land Pollution and Degradation

As per study conducted by National Bureau of Soil Survey and Land Use Planning, Nagpur, [a Regional Centre of Indian Council of Agricultural Research (ICAR)], an area of about 146.82 million hectares is subjected to various kinds of land degradation, viz. water and wind erosion, water logging, alkalinity/salinity, soil acidity and other complex problems across the country. Frequent events of droughts, floods and climate change also have an impact on soil fertility and land degradation, thereby affecting foodgrains production in the country.

Land, a non-renewable resource, is central to all primary production systems. Over the years, India's landmass has suffered from different types of degradations. Floods and droughts are recurrent phenomena in India, severely constraining agriculture. The problem of land degradation gets exacerbated due to large scale land erosion in which fertile top soil is lost.

Land degradation occurring due to the natural and human induced causes, like wind erosion and water logging, is one of the priority concerns in India. The varying degrees and types of degradation stem mainly from unsustainable use and inappropriate land management practices.

1.2.1 Industrial Effluents: Soil pollution from heavy metals due to improper disposal of industrial effluents, along with the excessive use of pesticides and mismanagement of domestic and municipal wastes, is becoming a major concern. Though no reliable estimates are available to depict the exact extent and degree of this type of land degradation, it is believed that the problem is extensive and its effects are significant. Some commercial fertilizers also contain appreciable quantities of heavy metals, which have undesirable effects on the environment. The indiscriminate use of agrochemicals, such as fertilizers and pesticides, is often responsible for land degradation.

1.2.2 Pressure of Human and Cattle Population: In addition to the wastelands, other areas such as deserts, drought-prone, flood-prone and tribal areas have been subjected to severe forms of degradation. The capacity of these lands is limited due to environmental factors. Pressures of human and livestock population have further compromised them.

1.2.3 Community Lands: Some of the most degraded lands in the country are the common property resources (CPRs). CPRs are resources on which people have an equal right of use. These resources include community pastures, community forests, wastelands and common dumping and threshing grounds. In spite of concerted efforts to check deforestation and the various afforestation schemes taken up during successive Five Year Plans, large tracks of forest continue to be classified as degraded.

1.2.4 Intensive Agricultural Practices: Intensive agricultural practices that rely heavily on water, chemical fertilisers and pesticides have caused water-logging and salinity in many parts of the country. The expansion of the irrigation system without adequate steps for treatment of the catchment areas has exacerbated this. The quest for increased agricultural productivity has led to intensive cultivation of marginal lands causing their degradation.

1.2.5 Unsanitary Disposal of Solid Wastes: Pollution of land results also from the unsanitary disposal of solid wastes. In India open dumping of such wastes of municipal and industrial origin on low lying land is a common phenomenon. This serves as a breeding ground for pests and disease carrying vectors.

1.2.6 Mining Activities: Land degradation is considered to be unavoidable by-product of mining and has reached alarming proportions, mainly due to over-exploitation and mismanagement of natural resources. Mining activity often leads to environmental problems like land degradation, particularly in opencast mining and land subsidence in underground mining. Open-cast mining in areas with forest cover causes deforestation.

1.2.7 Other Causes: Other important factors responsible for large-scale degradation are the following:

1. Non-adoption of adequate soil conservation measures.
2. Improper crop rotation.
3. Indiscriminate use of agro-chemicals such as fertilizers and pesticides.
4. Improper planning and management of irrigation systems.
5. Extraction of groundwater in excess of the recharge capacity.
6. Extension of cultivation to lands of low potential or high

natural hazards.

In addition, there are a few underlying or indirect pressures such as land shortage, short-term or insecure land tenancy, open access resource, economic status and poverty of the agriculture dependent people which are also instrumental, to a significant extent, for the degradation of land.

1.3 Consequences of Land Degradation

Land degradation has a direct bearing on the productivity of soil, its vulnerability to rainfall variations, scarcity of drinking water, fodder and fuel wood. Given the inter-linkages of crop production, livestock economy and environment, land degradation has a major impact on the livelihoods of the people, especially in rural areas.

The increasing generation of solid waste is a growing problem in all cities. Uncollected garbage is not only visually ugly, it also causes diseases. Dumping garbage into landfills is not an attractive option in land scarce cities and should be minimised. Most industrial countries now require their citizens to segregate wastes at home into recyclable products. Cities and towns must be encouraged to evolve systems with citizen participation, for segregation of waste at point of origin, maximising recycling and safe disposal of the rest. India's villages also have a huge problem of garbage disposal which must be addressed through self-help groups (SHGs) and panchayti raj institutions (PRIs).

Direct consequences of agricultural development on the environment arise from intensive farming activities, which contribute to soil erosion, land salination and loss of nutrients. The introduction of *green revolution* in the country has been accompanied by over-exploitation of land and water resources and excessive usage of fertilizers and pesticides. Shifting cultivation has also been a major factor responsible for land degradation in hilly areas. Leaching due to extensive use of pesticides and fertilizers is a major source of contamination of water bodies.

The extent of agricultural intensification and extensification is characterized by an increase in cropping and irrigation intensity and the unbalanced use of chemical fertilizers, pesticides and insecticides. It has also led to land degradation, overexploitation of underground water resources and increased use of chemical fertilizers, leading to eutrophication and water pollution in some regions.

Enhanced intensification and extensification also leads to salination, alkalization and water logging in irrigated areas, along with eutrophication of water bodies and ill health of oceans, leading to loss of biodiversity. For achieving and maintaining food security and sustainable forestry, controlling of land/soil erosion is extremely vital. It is essential to control soil erosion in order to attain and maintain food security, sustainable forestry and agricultural and rural development.

1.4 Strategies to Check Land Degradation

The prevention of land degradation and the augmentation of the carrying capacity of land to provide food, fuel and fodder requirements have, therefore, been a primary concern of the Government. Special Area Development Programmes have been funded to mitigate the harsh living conditions of people through better land management, water harvesting and conservation practices on a watershed basis.

India has paid a good deal of attention to harness its water resources by way of construction of major, medium and minor irrigation projects and the development of ground water resources. Organizations have also been set up in this field, namely Central and State Irrigation Departments, Central Water Commission and the Central Ground Water Board. However, very little attention has been paid to the proper management of land and soil resources with the result that they have suffered very serious degradation. The losses which the country is bearing on account of the continuing degradation of its land resources are of staggering dimensions and constitute one of the important threats to India's economic progress.

Land degradation problem could be tackled to an extent by suitable policies that would internalize the issue into proper decision-making. At the macro level, the existing database on land use statistics cannot adequately facilitate the analysis of land degradation and its impact. Changes in the classification of land use statistics are needed in order to study its impact. Advanced technology like remote sensing could go a long way in generating vital information on different dimensions of land degradation.

The information base on which farmers make decisions is incomplete in terms of internalizing rapid changes in soil and water quality variables. Hence, there is the need to move towards more sustainable practices such as integrated pest management and land-conserving crop rotations. Research needs to be focused on measures such as integrated crop management. An integrated approach to the problem of degradation, linking agriculture and environment, is yet to be attempted even at the policy level.

Overuse of resources has been identified as a major cause of land degradation. Creation of forest/biomass resources in all the culturable vacant lands should be taken up for strengthening life support system of communities and maintaining soil/water regimes.

1.5 Development of Wastelands

Land is the most important natural resource upon which all human activity is based. Man's inexorable progress towards development has, however, considerably damaged land resource base. Land suffers from various kinds of soil erosion, degradation and deforestation. To harness the full potential of the available land resources and prevent its further degradation, wasteland development is of great significance. The problem of degraded land and its management is complex and multi-dimensional and its development requires a scientific, holistic and innovative approach.

To accelerate the pace of development of wastelands and

degraded lands and to focus attention in this regard, the Government had set up the National Wastelands Development Board in 1985 under the Ministry of Environment and Forests. Later, a separate Department of Wastelands Development in the Ministry of Rural Development and Poverty Alleviation was created in 1992 and the National Wastelands Development Board was transferred to it. In April 1999, Department of Wastelands Development was renamed as the Department of Land Resources to act as the nodal agency for land resource management. Consequently, all land-based development programmes and the land reforms division were brought under this Department.

1.5.1 Wastelands Atlas, 2010: Wastelands can be defined as "degraded lands which can be brought under vegetative cover with reasonable efforts and which are currently underutilized, and also the land which is deteriorating for lack of appropriate water and soil management or on account of natural causes". Several agencies have estimated the extent of wastelands in India. However, these figures vary considerably—ranging between 30 million hectares and 175 million hectares, partly because of the varied definitions of wastelands.

Updation of Wasteland Atlas was initiated in 2003 to monitor changes in wastelands. National Remote Sensing Agency (NRSA) carried out mapping of wastelands across the country. To monitor the changes in the status of wastelands during the period 2003 and 2005-06, a project titled, "National Wasteland Monitoring" using Resourcesat-1 LISS III data was initiated in 2006. As per estimates arrived through this exercise, the total wastelands in the country stood at 47.22 million hectares accounting for 14.91 percent of the total geographical area of the country as per *Wasteland Atlas, 2010.*

A study titled *Comprehensive Assessment of Watershed Programmes in India* was assigned to the International Crops Research Institute for Semi-Arid Tropics (ICRISAT), Hyderabad, to critically assess the impact of various watershed development programmes in India and to identify the positive factors leading to reduction of wastelands by about 8.58

million hectares over a period of 5 years as indicated by *Wastelands Atlases* brought out in 2000 and 2005.

Main conclusions of the study were as under:

1. Targeted interventions to benefit the vulnerable groups enhanced the impact, sustainability of the programmes through development of social capital.
2. Vast scope exists to enhance the benefits and doubling the productivity of rain-fed areas by upgrading watershed programmes in the country with sustained and increased investments.

1.5.2 Integrated Watershed Management Programme (IWMP): The Ministry of Rural Development, Government of India, set up a Technical Committee (Chairman: S. Parthasarathy) in 2005 on the following 3 area development programmes then in existence: Drought Prone Areas Programme (DPAP) [1], Desert Development Programme (DDP) [2] and Integrated Wastelands Development Programme (IWDP). [3] These programmes were implemented in a project-based approach in a watershed, which is a geo-hydrological unit draining into a common point, for in-situ soil and water conservation, afforestation etc. The Committee was asked to address major issues in watershed programmes and recommend viable strategies and mechanisms for strengthening implementation of these programmes.

The Committee held wide-ranging discussions with State Governments, reputed NGOs and institutions, visited a number of watershed projects and held discussions on project sites with village communities to formulate recommendations. Based on the recommendations of the Committee, it was decided to integrate and consolidate the above-mentioned 3 area development programmes of the Ministry of Rural Development into a single programme called Integrated Watershed Management Programme (IWMP). This consolidation was for optimum use of resources, sustainable outcomes and integrated planning. The common guidelines for the watershed development projects were finalized and became operational with effect from April 1, 2008.

1.5.3 Technology Development Extension and Training (TDET) Scheme: This scheme was launched in 1993-94 to promote the development of cost effective and proven technologies for reclamation of various categories of wasteland land. Objectives of the scheme include the following:

1. Development of a database for wastelands.
2. Operationalisation of appropriate, cost effective and proven technologies for development of various categories of wastelands.
3. Dissemination of research finding and appropriate technologies for promoting wasteland development.

The scheme is being implemented through institutes of Indian Council of Agricultural Research (ICAR), state agricultural universities, District Rural Development Agencies (DRDAs) and government institutions with adequate institutional framework and organizational back up. Successful implementation of the scheme is expected to bridge the gap between existing technologies relevant to the latest situation for development of non-forest wasteland and wider application by organizations and agencies dealing with land based programme.

Under the scheme, 100 percent grant is admissible to implement projects on wastelands owned by government, public sector undertakings, universities, panchayats etc. In case projects include the development of wastelands of private farmers and corporate bodies, the project cost is to be shared 60:40 between government and beneficiaries.

Important activities under the scheme include the following:

1. Development of database on wastelands.
2. Promotion and testing of various agro-forestry models in different agro-climatic zones of the country.
3. Test effective technologies for increasing the productivity of saline and alkaline soils.
4. Promotion of medicinal and herbal plantations of non-forest wastelands.

5. Composite technologies for water harvesting.
6. Treatment of degraded lands through bio-fertilisers.
7. Development of technology for jojaoba plantation in arid and semi-arid areas through Israeli collaboration.

Technical brochures have been brought out on different technologies that could be adopted for development of different categories of problem lands.

Some of the innovative projects that have been taken up under the Scheme are as under:

1. In collaboration with National Remote Sensing Agency (NRSA), Hyderabad, a detailed exercise has been undertaken to digitally map and prioritize watersheds in 3 states on the basis of different thematic layers like land use, soil type, water availability etc. on a pilot basis. This information could be usefully employed to identify watersheds for development as per priority.
2. Indian Institute of Technology (IIT), Delhi has undertaken a pilot project and evolved a low-cost technology to convert domestic and farm waste into bio-fertilizers and successfully used the bio-fertilizer in growing fruit trees in public wastelands in Haryana and Rajasthan.
3. Gujarat Institute of Desert Ecology, Bhuj has developed an integrated model for reclamation of saline lands in the Rann of Kutch region that included suitable agro-forestry species, water conservation and land reclamation measurers.
4. The Forest Development Agency, Solan, Himachal Pradesh has successfully demonstrated the usefulness of a people participatory model in reclaiming forest wastelands through cultivation of medicinal plants and facilitating necessary linkages for marketing and processing the produce so that sustainable livelihoods are provided to the beneficiaries involved.
5. The Minor Irrigation Department, Sangli, Maharashtra has completed a pilot project in executing a sub-surface drainage system in waterlogged and saline lands of

Dudhgaon village. With this, the waterlogged areas—that remained unused for decades due to severe salinity—have successfully been reclaimed and the beneficiary farmers have reported that these lands have not only been brought under plough but also are yielding substantial returns just within a year of cultivation.

1.6 Schemes for Treatment of Degraded Lands

With a view to prevent land degradation and to sustain agricultural production, Department of Agriculture and Cooperation of the Ministry of Agriculture, Government of India is implementing various soil and water conservation programmes for treatment/reclamation of degraded lands. The objectives of various schemes/programmes are as under:

1. Implementation of soil and water conservation programmes for the prevention of soil erosion and land degradation in order to sustain agriculture production on watershed approach basis.
2. Formulation of policies and strategies to address the issues regarding sustainable agriculture in the context of risks associated with climate change and suggesting appropriate adaptation and mitigation measures to combat adverse effect of climate change on agriculture production including natural resources.
3. Reclamation and development of land affected by alkalinity and acidity.
4. Providing scientific database on soil and land uses for watershed planning and programme implementation.
5. Prevention of runoff and premature siltation of the reservoirs, thereby sustaining irrigation potential and water storage capacity of the various reservoirs across the country.
6. Encouraging settled cultivation in lieu of shifting cultivation among the Jhumia families of the States of North East Region and restoration of ecology and checking land degradation.

7. Creation of employment opportunities and improving the socio-economic conditions of the rural community.
8. Development of human resources through training and capacity building programmes of state officials working in the area of soil and water conservation.

The Central Sector Schemes and Centrally Sponsored Programmes being implemented by the Government are described below.

1.6.1 Soil and Land Use Survey of India (SLUSI): SLUSI is a subordinate office of the Department of Agriculture and Cooperation, established in the year 1958 with its headquarters in New Delhi. SLUSI has 7 Regional Centres located at NOIDA (Uttar Pradesh), Kolkata, Bengaluru, Nagpur, Hyderabad, Ahmedabad and Ranchi. The major mandate of SLUSI is to conduct various types of soil and land resource surveys and provide a soil-related database for the planning and implementation of programmes relating to soil and water conservation for the development of degraded lands. The main activities of SLUSI are the following:

1. Rapid Reconnaissance Survey (RRS) of the catchments of river valley projects and flood prone rivers for categorization of watersheds.
2. Detailed Soil Survey (DSS) of selected *very high* and *high* priority watersheds to provide a sound database for execution of soil conservation measures as well as for scientific land use planning.
3. Soil Resource Mapping (SRM).
4. Development of GIS-based Web Server.
5. Organizing short training courses on soil surveys and data use for planning of watershed management.
6. Consultancy projects in soil mapping.

The organization is engaged in conducting soil surveys to provide database for land-based developmental programmes for the user organizations. Besides, SLUSI provides training to the State officials drawn from the state departments such as agriculture, soil conservation, soil survey, forestry and irrigation.

1.6.2 Soil Conservation Training Centre, Damodar Valley Corporation (DVC), Hazaribagh, Jharkhand: This Centre organizes medium and short duration training courses every year for field functionaries and project officers of the State Governments engaged in implementation of soil and water conservation programmes.

1.6.3 Soil Conservation in the Catchments of River Valley Projects and Flood Prone Rivers: Presently, this Centrally-sponsored programme is being implemented in 60 catchments of 27 States (all the States except Goa) including all the States of North Eastern Region of the country. The total catchment area of ongoing programme is about 113.51 million hectares, out of which an area about 30.15 million hectares is categorized as a priority area, needing urgent treatment under this programme. The catchments are mostly inter-state in nature and all categories of lands viz. agriculture, waste lands and forests are taken up for treatment in an integrated manner on watershed approach basis. The main objectives are the following:

1. Prevention of land degradation by adopting a multi-disciplinary integrated approach for soil conservation and watershed management in catchment areas.
2. Improvement of land capability and moisture regime in the watersheds.
3. Promotion of land uses to match land capability.
4. Prevention of runoff and premature siltation of the reservoirs, thereby sustaining irrigation potential and water storage capacity of the various reservoirs across the country.

Under this programme, various soil and water conservation measures are implemented on watershed approach. With a view to assess the impact of soil and water conservation measures, a system of continuous monitoring of rainfall, runoff and sediment parameters prior to, during and after treatment of the watershed are collected and analyzed for assessing the impact of watershed interventions. For this purpose, an amount of 3 percent of the allocated funds are earmarked for meeting the cost of establishment of Sediment Monitoring Stations (SMS) and also to meet the operational cost of these SMSs.

1.6.4 Reclamation and Development of Alkali and Acid Soils (RADAS): This Programme was restructured and launched during Eleventh Five Year Plan (2007-12) for development of alkali and acid soils in the states of Arunachal Pradesh, Mizoram, Gujarat, Haryana, Punjab, Karnataka and Rajasthan.

The Programme aims at improving physical conditions and the productivity status of alkali and acid soils for restoring optimum crop production. The major components permissible under the programme are on farm development, viz. land levelling, bunding, community drainage systems, application of soil amendments, organic manures, crop/horticultural/fuel wood production etc.

1.6.5 Watershed Development Project in Shifting Cultivation Areas: This Scheme was launched during the Eighth Five Year Plan (1992-1997) in 7 states of North Eastern Region, namely Arunachal Pradesh, Assam, Manipur, Meghalaya, Mizoram, Nagaland and Tripura with 100 percent Special Central Assistance to the State Plan. The major objectives of the scheme are the following:

1. Protection of hill slopes of Jhum areas through soil and water conservation measures on a watershed basis to reduce further land degradation.
2. Encouragement and assistance to Jhumia families to develop Jhum land for productive uses with improved cultivation and suitable package of practices leading to settled cultivation.
3. Improvement of the socio-economic status of Jhumia families through household/land based activities.
4. Mitigation of the ill effects of shifting cultivation by introducing appropriate land use methods through improved technologies.

Under this scheme, treatment of arable and non-arable land through drainage line treatment, water harvesting structures, farm ponds, horticulture, afforestation, silvipasture, crop demonstration etc. are taken up.

1.6.6 National Mission for Sustainable Agriculture (NMSA): NMSA is one of the 8 Missions under the National Action Plan on Climate Change (NAPCC). It seeks to address issues regarding sustainable agriculture in the context of risks associated with climate change by devising appropriate adaptation and mitigation strategies for ensuring food security, enhancing livelihood opportunities and contributing to economical stability at the national level.

NMSA identifies 10 key dimensions for promoting sustainable agricultural practices, which will be realized by implementing a Programme of Action that covers both adaptation and mitigation measures through 4 functional areas, namely research and development, technologies, products and practices, infrastructure and capacity building. While recognizing the role of modern technologies and research in promoting the sustainability of agricultural production, NMSA also emphasizes the need to harness traditional knowledge and agricultural heritage for insitu conservation of genetic resources.

End Notes

1. **Drought Prone Areas Programme (DPAP):** DPAP was the earliest area development programme launched by the Central Government in 1973-74 to tackle the special problems faced by those fragile areas, which were constantly affected by severe drought conditions. These areas were characterized by large human and cattle populations which were continuously putting heavy pressure on the already degraded natural resources for food, fodder and fuel. The major problems were: (a) continuous depletion of vegetative cover, (b) increase in soil erosion, and (c) fall in ground water levels due to continuous exploitation without any effort to recharge the underground aquifers.

   The basic objective of the programme was to minimize the adverse impacts of drought on the production of crops and livestock and productivity of land, water and human resources, thereby ultimately leading to the drought proofing of the affected areas. The programme aimed at promoting overall economic development and improving the socio-economic condition of the resource poor and disadvantaged sections inhabiting the programme areas through creation, widening and equitable distribution of the resource base and increased employment opportunities. The objectives of the programme were addressed in general by taking up development works through watershed approach for land development, water resource development and afforestation/pasture development.

2. **Desert Development Programme (DDP):** DDP was started both in hot desert areas of Rajasthan, Gujarat and Haryana and the cold deserts of Jammu & Kashmir and Himachal Pradesh in 1977-78. From 1995-96, the coverage was extended to a few more districts in Andhra Pradesh and Karnataka.

   The programme was conceived as a long-term measure for restoration of ecological balance by conserving, developing and harnessing land, water, livestock and human resources. It sought to promote the economic development of the village community and improve the economic conditions of the resource poor and disadvantaged sections of society in the rural areas.

3. **Integrated Wastelands Development Programme (IWDP):** IWDP, a Centrally-sponsored Programme, was under implementation since 1989-90. From April 1, 1995, the programme was implemented through watershed approach under the common guidelines for watershed development. The development of wastelands and degraded lands under the programme was intended to promote the generation of employment in rural areas besides enhancing the participation of people at all stages, leading to sustainable development of land and equitable sharing of the benefits. IWDP envisaged the development of non-forests wastelands in the country.

2

Institutional Framework for Agriculture

Agricultural sector occupies a key position in the Indian economy. It provides employment to about 60 percent of the working population of India. Around 15 percent of India's national income originates from the agricultural sector. It is imperative that the problems of farmers are addressed with a sense of urgency. Agriculture being a State subject, the bulk of public investment in agriculture takes place at the level of States and the Central Government supports the States as a catalyst.

Agricultural products like cereals (mainly rice), tea, coffee, cashew, spices, tobacco and leather are important items of India's exports and hence foreign exchange earnings. Agriculture is also the source of raw material for agro-based industries including textiles, cigarettes, jute, sugar, paper, processed foodstuffs and *vanaspati*. Moreover, agricultural sector provides market for capital goods (tractors, pump sets and other agricultural machinery), inputs (fertilisers, insecticides), and light consumer goods. The nation has invested huge resources for the development of agriculture under various plans.

The development of the agricultural sector depends, to a large extent, on such core industries as power, petroleum, fertilisers and machine tools. Thus, there is inter-dependence between agriculture and industry.

Agriculture being a state subject, the primary responsibility for increasing agriculture production, enhancing productivity, and exploring the vast untapped potential of the sector rests with the State Governments. However, in order to supplement the efforts of the State Governments, a number of Centrally-sponsored and Central Sector schemes are being implemented for enhancing agricultural production and productivity in the country and increasing the income of the farming community.

2.1 Agriculture in the Constitution of India

Agriculture is a State subject according to Entry 14 in State List (List II) of the Seventh Schedule to the Constitution of India. Though agriculture as such figures in the State List yet certain aspects of agriculture fall in Union List/Concurrent List (List I/List III). Thus, fisheries belong to the State List (Entry 21) but fishing and fisheries beyond territorial waters belong to the Union List (Entry 57).

Similarly, animal husbandry and veterinary training are State subjects (Entry 15) but prevention of cruelty to animals is a concurrent subject (Entry 17). Forestry and protection of wild animals and birds originally belonged to State List (Entries 18 and 20). However, they were transferred to the Concurrent List (Entries 17A and 17B) through the Constitution (Forty-second Amendment) Act, 1976.

The enlargement of Entry 33 in the Concurrent List through the Constitution (Third Amendment) Act, 1954 made agriculture virtually a concurrent subject. It reads as follows: "Trade and commerce in, and the production, supply and distribution of: (a) the products of any industry where the control of such industry by the Union is declared by Parliament by law to be expedient in the public interest, and imported goods of the same kind as such products; (b) foodstuffs, including edible oilseeds and oils; (c) cattle fodder, including oilcakes and other concentrates; (d) raw cotton, whether ginned or unginned and cotton seeds; and (e) raw jute." Thus, trade, commerce, production, supply and distribution of foodstuffs including edible oils and oil seeds are covered by the Concurrent List.

Water and power development is another important area of State activity subject to Central control. Water supplies, irrigation and canals, drainage and embankments, water storage and water power belong to the State List (Entry 17) but these are subject to the provisions of the Union List (Entry 56) which deals with the regulation and development of inter-State rivers and river valleys. Since electricity belongs to Concurrent List (Entry 38), the Centre's concurrent jurisdiction on water power is automatic.

2.2 Ministry of Agriculture

The nodal agency for development of agriculture in India is the Ministry of Agriculture, Government of India.

2.2.1 Departments of the Ministry: It has three departments: (a) Department of Agriculture and Co-operation, (b) Department of Animal Husbandry, Dairying and Fisheries, and (c) Department of Agricultural Research and Education.

A. Department of Agriculture and Co-operation: It deals with such matters as crops, horticulture, seeds, integrated nutrient management, plant protection, mechanization and technology, agriculture marketing, information technology, drought management, and agricultural census.

B. Department of Animal Husbandry, Dairying and Fisheries: This Department is responsible for matters relating to livestock production, preservation, protection and improvement of stocks, dairy development, matters relating to the Delhi Milk Scheme and the National Dairy Development Board. It also looks after all matters pertaining fisheries, which includes inland and marine sectors and matters related to the National Fisheries Development Board.

The Department advises the State Governments/Union Territories in the formulation of policies and programmes in the field of animal husbandry, dairy development and fisheries. The main focus of the activities is on: (a) development of requisite infrastructure in States/UTs for improving animal productivity, (b) promoting infrastructure for handling, processing and marketing of milk and milk products, (c) preservation and protection of livestock through provision of health care, (d) strengthening of central livestock farms (cattle, sheep and poultry) for development of superior germplasm for distribution to States, and (e) expansion of aquaculture in fresh and brackish water, development of marine fisheries infrastructure and post-harvest operations and welfare of fisherfolk etc.

C. Department of Agricultural Research and Education (DARE): DARE coordinates and promotes agricultural research and education in the country. DARE provides the necessary government linkages for the Indian Council of Agricultural Research (ICAR), the premier research organisation with a scientific strength of about 25,000 and a countrywide network of 49 Institutes, 6 National Bureaux, 18 National Research Centres, 24 Project Directorates, 89 All-India Co-ordinated Research Projects and 45 Agriculture Universities spread all over the country.

DARE is the nodal agency for international co-operation in the area of agricultural research and education in India. It liaises with foreign governments, UN, and other multilateral agencies for cooperation in various areas of agricultural research. It also coordinates admissions of foreign students in various Indian agriculture universities/ICAR Institutes.

The major functions of DARE are the following:

1. To look after all aspects of the agricultural research and Education (including horticulture, natural resources management, agriculture engineering, agricultural extension, animal science, economic statics and marketing and fisheries) involving coordination between the central and state agencies.
2. To attend all matters relating to Indian Council of Agricultural Research.
3. To attend all matters concerning the development of new technology in agriculture, horticulture, natural resources management, agriculture engineering, agricultural extension, animal science, economic statistics and marketing and fisheries, including such functions as plant and animal introduction and exploration and soil and land use survey and planning.
4. International co-operation in the field of agricultural research and education including relations with foreign

and international agricultural research and educational institutions and organisations, including participation in international conferences, associations and other bodies dealing with agricultural research and education and follow-up decisions at such international conferences etc.

5. Fundamental, applied and operational research and higher education including co-ordination of such research and higher education in agriculture including agro-forestry, animal husbandry, dairying, fisheries, agricultural statistics, economics and marketing.

2.3 Important Organisations under the Ministry of Agriculture

2.3.1 Indian Council of Agricultural Research (ICAR): ICAR is an autonomous organisation under the Department of Agricultural Research and Education (DARE), Ministry of Agriculture, Government of India. Formerly known as Imperial Council of Agricultural Research, it was established on July 16, 1929 as a registered society under the Societies Registration Act, 1860 in pursuance of the report of the Royal Commission on Agriculture. The ICAR has its headquarters in New Delhi.

ICAR is the apex body for co-ordinating, guiding and managing research and education in agriculture including horticulture, fisheries and animal sciences in the entire country. It is one of the largest national agricultural systems in the world.

ICAR has played a pioneering role in ushering Green Revolution and subsequent developments in agriculture in India through its research and technology development, thus making a visible impact on the national food and nutritional security. It has played a major role in promoting excellence in higher education in agriculture. It is engaged in cutting edge areas of science and technology development and its scientists are internationally acknowledged in their fields.

2.3.2 Commission for Agricultural Costs and Prices (CACP): The Agricultural Prices Commission was set up in

January 1965 to advise the Government on price policy of major agricultural commodities with a view to evolving a balance and integrated price structure in the perspective of the overall needs of the economy and with due regard to the interests of the producer and the consumer. Since March 1985, the Commission has been known as Commission for Agricultural Costs and Prices (CACP).

CACP is composed of a Chairman, a Member Secretary, two official members and three non-official members. The non-official members are representatives of the farming community. They are usually persons with long field experience and active association with the farming community.

Assurance of a remunerative and stable price environment is considered very important for increasing agricultural production and productivity since the market place for agricultural produce tends to be inherently unstable, which often inflict undue losses on the growers, even when they adopt the best available technology package and produce efficiently. Towards this end, minimum support prices (MSPs) for major agricultural products are fixed by the government, each year, after taking into account the recommendations of CACP.

2.3.3 National Seeds Corporation (NSC): Working since 1963, under the control of the Ministry of Agriculture of the Government of India. NSC undertakes production, processing and marketing of agricultural seeds. Its product range includes cereals, pulses, oilseeds, fodder, fibre and vegetable crops.

NSC pioneered the development of Indian seed industry on scientific lines with its involvement in the formulation of seed certification standards. Its seeds are evaluated for quality standards by independent seed certification agencies besides internal quality checks and laboratory tests in its own seed testing laboratories located in Delhi, Secunderabad, Pune, Bhopal and Kolkata.

To meet the twin challenges of providing food and nutritional security to the people, agriculture production (especially of the foodgrains crops) has to be increased on sustained basis so as to achieve self-sufficiency in all major crops like cereals, pulses, oilseeds, fibres and fodder etc. For achieving the above objectives, seed is one of the critical inputs besides other inputs like fertilizers, irrigation, plant protection, farm practices etc. With the help of ICAR, NSC has been in the business of multiplication and production of seeds of all major crops. NSC is the single largest producer of certified seeds in the country in terms of quantity and third largest company in terms of turnover amongst all the seed producing companies including private sector companies.

NSC ensures to provide quality seeds of high yielding varieties and hybrids of all major cereal crops like paddy, wheat, maize, pulses, and oilseeds.

Apart from this main Ministry, there are at least 7 other Ministries of the Government of India which deal, in one way or the other, with subjects related to agriculture and allied activities. These are the following:

1. Ministry of Water Resources.
2. Ministry of Rural Development.
3. Ministry of Chemicals and Fertilizers.
4. Ministry of Food Processing Industries.
5. Ministry of Consumer Affairs, Food and Public Distribution.
6. Ministry of Panchayati Raj.
7. Ministry of Environment and Forests

2.4 National Agriculture Policy (NAP), 2000

On July 28, 2000, Government of India announced a National Agriculture Policy to include this vital sector of the economy in the ambit of economic reforms. After the economic reforms in 1991-92 that removed the restrictive and protective licensing regime for industry, the policy focus turned to agriculture. There was the general impression that agriculture in India operated amidst a number of restraints and controls and that farmers did not receive the benefits of free trade as compared to other sectors of the economy. The main elements of NAP, 2000 were the following:

1. Private sector investment in agriculture would be encouraged, particularly in areas like agricultural research, human resource development, post harvest management and marketing.
2. Catapulting agricultural growth to over 4 percent per annum by 2005.
3. Restrictions on the movement of agricultural commodities throughout the country would be progressively dismantled.
4. Appropriate measures would be adopted to ensure that agriculturists by and large, remain outside the regulatory and tax collection system.
5. Rural electrification would be given high priority as a prime mover for agricultural development.
6. Progressive institutionalisation of rural and farm credit would be continued for providing timely and adequate credit to farmers.

2.5 National Policy for Farmers, 2007

National Commission on Farmers (NCF) [Chairman: M.S. Swaminathan] was set up in 2004 to suggest an action plan for farmers and farm sector. The Commission submitted five Reports between December 2005 and October 2006. Main recommendations of the Commission included the following:

1. Asset reforms covering land, water, livestock and bio-resources.
2. Farmer-friendly support services covering extension, training and knowledge, connectivity, credit and insurance.
3. Assured and remunerative marketing.
4. Inputs and delivery services.
5. Curriculum reforms in the agriculture universities.
6. Bringing agriculture in the Concurrent List of the Constitution.
7. Setting up of a National Food Security and Sovereignty Board.
8. Universalization of public distribution system (PDS).

9. Setting up of an Indian Trade Organization.
10. Converting Commission on Agriculture Costs and Prices into an autonomous statutory organization.
11. Minimum support prices (MSPs) for agricultural commodities to be at least 50 percent more than the cost of production.
12. Launching a Rural Non-farm Livelihood Initiative (RNFLI).

The NCF prepared, along with its final report, a draft National Policy for Farmers incorporating its main recommendations. Based on the draft prepared by the NCF and after consultations with State Governments and the Central Ministries concerned, Government of India approved the National Policy for Farmers, 2007. The primary focus of this policy is on 'farmer' defined holistically and not merely on agriculture. In that sense, it is much more comprehensive than an Agriculture Policy. The objective, *inter alia*, is to improve the economic viability of farming through substantially improving net income of farmers. There is emphasis on increased productivity, profitability, institutional support, and improvement of land, water and support services apart from provisions of appropriate price policy, risk mitigation measures and so on.

2.6 Recent Schemes for Agricultural Development

2.6.1 Rashtriya Krishi Vikas Yojana (RKVY), 2007: Concerned by the slow growth in the agriculture and allied sectors, the National Development Council (NDC), in its meeting held on May 29, 2007 resolved that a special Additional Central Assistance Scheme. The NDC resolved that agricultural development strategies must be reoriented to meet the needs of farmers and called upon the Central and State governments to evolve a strategy to rejuvenate agriculture. The NDC reaffirmed its commitment to achieve 4 percent annual growth in the agricultural sector during the Eleventh Five Year Plan (2007-12).

A. Basic Objectives of RKVY: RKVY aims at achieving 4 percent annual growth in the agriculture sector during the Eleventh Plan period by ensuring a holistic development of agriculture and allied sectors. The main objectives of the scheme are:

- To incentivise the states so as to increase public investment in agriculture and allied sectors.
- To provide flexibility and autonomy to states in the process of planning and executing agriculture and allied sector schemes.
- To ensure the preparation of agriculture plans for the districts and the states based on agro-climatic conditions, availability of technology and natural resources.
- To ensure that the local needs/crops/priorities are better reflected in the agricultural plans of the states.
- To achieve the goal of reducing the yield gaps in important crops through focussed interventions.
- To maximize returns to the farmers in agriculture and allied sectors.
- To bring about quantifiable changes in the production and productivity of various components of agriculture and allied sectors by addressing them in a holistic manner.

B. Primary Strategic Relevance of the Scheme: RKVY Scheme is a State Plan scheme administered by the Union Ministry of Agriculture over and above its existing Centrally Sponsored Schemes. RKVY Scheme has been formulated with two strategic objectives in mind—first, to incentivize States to allocate more funds for agriculture and allied sectors and second, to focus States to generate additional growth in agriculture and allied sectors by better planning and undertaking appropriate growth oriented projects to achieve the goal. This is to be done by drawing up plans for their agriculture and allied sectors more comprehensively, by integrating livestock, poultry and fisheries reflecting needs/crops/priorities taking agro-climatic conditions, natural resource issues and technology into account. Funds under the scheme are provided to the States as 100 percent grant by the

Central Government.

Allocation of funds to States is dependent on additional resources committed by States for agriculture and allied sectors in their state plans and growth projected and generated. There are no prescriptions about the projects, schemes and other programmes to be undertaken by States under RKVY. The Scheme provides complete flexibility to States to choose what is best suited in their conditions to generate growth so as to enable the country to achieve 4 percent growth in agriculture and allied sectors during the Eleventh Plan.

RKVY is a transformational jump in evolution of agricultural development schemes from variegated schematic approach followed so far through diverse but strait-jacketed schemes to a completely new approach in agriculture planning by allowing the States to plan their strategy and design appropriate schemes to implement that strategy with complete flexibility in scheme designs and autonomy in its implementation.

RKVY has imparted definite momentum to the agriculture sector. Regular activities starved of resources, promising strategies languishing for lack of support, and limited opportunities for experimentation and innovation, have found a new hope in RKVY. States are allocating more funds to agriculture to take up schemes of agriculture development. This is reflected in additional plan allocation to agriculture sector. There is a sense of hope and optimism. Agriculture, which had slid back, is making a comeback. RKVY has accelerated revival of agriculture and put it on growth path.

2.6.2 Macro Management of Agriculture (MMA) Scheme: Agriculture is a state subject. Hence, the primary role for increasing productivity and production of food grains and other agriculture crops is that of the State Governments. However, in order to supplement the efforts of the State Governments, a number of Centrally-sponsored and Central Sector Schemes are being implemented for enhancement of agricultural productivity and production for livelihood security of the farming community and food security in the country.

MMA Scheme was launched in 2000-01 by integrating 27 centrally sponsored schemes moving away from a programmatic to a macro management mode of assistance to the states in the form of work plans prepared by the states and implemented in a spirit of partnership with the states. The scheme was conceived to be a step to provide sufficient autonomy and initiative to state governments to develop programmes and activities as per their felt needs and priorities. The scheme replaced the schematic rigid approach by a work-plan-based approach in an interactive mode to supplement and complement states' efforts in the agriculture sector.

MMA scheme was a major step towards decentralization, allowing states the flexibility to choose suitable interventions from the various components in addition to their own efforts towards growth of the agriculture sector. Later, with the launch of the National Horticulture Mission in 2005-06, 10 components relating to horticulture were excluded from the MMA scheme. Thus, the MMA scheme comprises the following 17 components or sub-schemes, focusing on rice, wheat, coarse cereals, sugarcane, soil health, nutrient and pest management, farm mechanization and watershed development:

1. Integrated Cereal Development Programmes in Rice Based Cropping System Areas.
2. Integrated Cereal Development Programmes in Wheat Based Cropping System Areas.
3. Integrated Cereal Development Programmes in Coarse Cereals Based Cropping System Areas.
4. Special Jute Development Programme.
5. Sustainable Development of Sugarcane Based Cropping System.
6. Balanced and Integrated Use of Fertilizer.
7. Promotion of Agricultural Mechanization among Small Farmers.
8. National Watershed Development Project for Rain-fed Areas.

9. Scheme for Foundation and Certified Seed Production of Vegetable Crops.
10. Soil Conservation in Catchments of River Valley Projects and Flood Prone Rivers.
11. Reclamation and Development of Alkali Soils.
12. State Land Use Board.
13. Assistance to Cooperatives of Weaker Section.
14. Assistance to Women Cooperatives.
15. Non-overdue Cover Scheme.
16. Agriculture Credit Stabilization Fund.
17. Special Scheme for SC/ST.

A. Revised MMA Scheme: In the year 2008-09, the MMA scheme was revised to improve its efficacy in supplementing/complementing the efforts of the States towards enhancement of agricultural production and productivity. Role of the Scheme was redefined to avoid overlapping and duplication of efforts and to make it more relevant to the present agricultural scenario in the States to achieve the basic objectives of food security and improving the livelihoods of rural masses. Revised MMA scheme comprised 11 sub-schemes relating to crop production and natural resource management. Further, one sub-scheme relating to State Land Use Board (SLUB) was discontinued with effect from August 1, 2009. The revised MMA scheme now comprises 10 sub-schemes, which are as under:

1. Integrated Cereal Development Programmes in Rice Based Cropping System Areas.
2. Integrated Cereal Development Programmes in Wheat Based Cropping System Areas.
3. Integrated Cereal Development Programmes in Coarse Cereals Based Cropping System Areas.
4. Integrated Development Programme for Pulses and Oilseeds (New Scheme included as one of the crop production programmes).
5. Sustainable Development of Sugarcane Based Cropping System.

6. Balanced and Integrated Use of Fertilizers.
7. Promotion of Agricultural Mechanization among Small Farmers.
8. National Watershed Development Project for Rain-fed Areas.
9. Soil Conservation in Catchments of River Valley Projects and Flood Prone Rivers.
10. Reclamation and Development of Alkali Soils.

The salient features of the revised MMA Scheme are as follows:

1. Practice of allocating funds to States/UTs on historical basis has been replaced by a new allocation criteria based on gross cropped area and area under small and marginal holdings.
2. Assistance under MMA would be provided to the States/UTs as 100 percent grant.
3. Subsidy structure has been aligned to make subsidy pattern uniform under all the schemes implemented by the Department of Agriculture and Cooperation. Revised subsidy norms indicate the maximum permissible limit of assistance. States have freedom to retain existing norms, or increase them to a reasonable level provided that the same do not exceed the specified revised upper limits.
4. Two new components have been added namely: (a) Pulses and oilseeds crop production programmes for the areas not covered under the Integrated Scheme of Oilseeds, Pulses, Oil palm and Maize (ISOPOM), and (b) "Reclamation of Acidic Soil" to the existing component of "Reclamation of Alkali Soil".
5. Ceiling for new initiatives has been increased from existing 10 percent to 20 percent of the allocation.
6. At least 33 percent of the funds have to be earmarked for small, marginal and women farmers.
7. Active participation of the panchayati raj institutions (PRIs) of all tiers has to be ensured in the implementation of the revised MMA scheme including review, monitoring

and evaluation at district/sub-district level.

2.6.3 Extending Green Revolution to the Eastern States: This programme envisages adoption of new seed varieties, farm machinery, integrated nutrient and pest management, and knowledge-based interventions developed for different agro-climatic zones. The programme is under implementation in Bihar, Chhattisgarh, Jharkhand, Eastern Uttar Pradesh, West Bengal and Odisha. Recently, the state of Assam has also been included under this initiative.

2.6.4 Support to State Extension Programmes for Extension Reforms: The objective of the Scheme is to make the extension system farmer-driven and farmer-accountable by way of new institutional arrangements for technology dissemination. 598 Agricultural Technology Management Agencies (ATMAs) have been established at district level to operationalize the extension reforms. The scheme was modified in 2010 to provide for the following activities:

- Provision of specialist and functionary support at different levels.
- Innovative support through a 'Farmer Friend' at village level.
- Revision in ATMA Cafeteria.
- Farmers' Advisory Committees at State, District and Block levels.

2.6.5 Agricultural Technology Management Agency (ATMA): ATMA is a district level body created under the ITD component of NATP for pilot testing agricultural extension reforms. This is an autonomous institution with participation of all the key stakeholders involved in agricultural activities for sustainable agricultural development. It has the flexibility to receive funds directly from Central and State Governments, membership fees, beneficiaries' contribution etc. ATMA has the main responsibility of all the technology dissemination activities at the district level. It has linkages with all the line departments, research organizations, non-governmental organizations and agencies associated with agricultural development in the district with a substantial representation of organizations of farmers.

Research and extension units within the district, such as department of agriculture, horticulture, animal husbandry, fisheries, sericulture, marketing etc. are constituent members.

3

Agrarian Structure, Farm Productivity and Social Justice

Agrarian structure is undoubtedly one of the most important determinants of farm efficiency. Therefore, it is believed that reorganization of agrarian structure is an essential and unavoidable necessity for agricultural development in an agrarian society like India, but its reorganization is a stupendous task. Agrarian structure does not merely relate to ownership of land, but in a broad sense, it includes the entire gamut of socio-economic structure of a pre-dominantly agrarian economy.

3.1 Pattern of Land Holdings

However, agrarian structure is developed over a period of time in regular and renewed basis to changing times and ever improving process of technological developments. The pattern of land holding and the emerging agricultural activities indeed hold key to the economic development of a country predominantly dependent on agriculture. Especially, the structure of land holding at any point of time has tremendous impact on the rural economy and rural population, whose livelihood and food security are directly influenced by the pattern of land structure and their management.

Therefore, if appropriately structured, it helps a society to attain rural economic growth and its equitable distribution. This is because there exists linkages between agrarian structure, agricultural growth and rural poverty. States where agrarian structure is more equitable, productivity is seen to be higher and poverty level appears to be lower/reduction of poverty tends to be higher. Needless to mention that, given a conducive agrarian structure, a high rate of exclusive growth of agriculture could considerably reduce the poverty levels.

Changes in agrarian structure (in order to be of optimum help to the society), are brought through land reforms keeping in view the production, distribution of the produce, pattern of land holding, tenancy structure and so on. Thus, agrarian structure is an institutional arrangement and the changes therein are primarily based on equity in distribution of land so as to enhance agricultural productivity.

However, in an agricultural economy, land under ownership holding is extremely fragmented with each family possessing a number of scattered tiny plots. Such type of land holding structure is adverse to management of land, use of irrigation, farm technology, and improved methods of cultivation. Precisely therefore, new farm technology, modern irrigation, application of new farm equipments and machinery may not be applied on such small and fragmented farm units and thus, it is not a suitable economic proposition, so far as production and productivity are concerned.

Similarly, large land holdings are prone to similar adverse situations and therefore, the big land holders tend to lease out a major portion of their holdings scattered in tiny plots due to lack of proper management and supervision, where the landlord may be interested only in appropriation of rent, but not in production/productivity. Further, he may be unwilling to invest in drainage, fencing, irrigation development, which could otherwise enhance production. Similarly, the tenant farmers in such a situation may be unwilling and ill-afford to make any investment owing to greater tenurial insecurity.

3.2 Skewed Distribution of Land

Despite some progressive (very limited) reforms in land at the all-India as well as state levels, inequitable distribution of land under ownership as well as operational holdings continues and is glaringly visible and adequately reflected in the NSS and Agricultural Census Reports released at different points of time. Such skewed distribution of land indeed is inimical to agricultural production, productivity, use of modern irrigation and farm technology. Thus, arises existence of numerically small number of large land holders having command over bulk of operated area vis-à-vis numerically large number of small land holders having command over lower proportion of the total operated area. Consequently, the debate (1960s) continues over the efficiency of small farms over the large ones on per acre productivity basis; and the so called 'inverse relation' between land size and productivity. [1]

Some argue that such a long debate in the late 1960s between two divergent groups of economists and the argument in favour of small farms based on higher productivity per acre, seems to have influenced the policy makers not to advocate progressive reforms in land to ensure equity (in distribution of land). [2] While one school of thought is of the opinion that tenancy rights and land distribution would lead to higher productivity and employment, the other group advocates expansion of large capitalized farms to cause efficient production conditions. But, the latter argument has the roots to believe that advent of *green revolution* has weakened the size-productivity relationship in favour of large farmers and also that, the small land holders are left behind as backward and inefficient.

The former group of economists argue in terms of lower efficiency of hired-labour based capitalist production relative to higher efficiency of family labour based peasant holdings. [3] The latter group of economists argue that in the emerging situation (owing to their ability to appropriate and retain surplus), the big land owner-cultivators are in a better position to invest more in the use of new farm technology, fixed capital and permanent development in land so as to get larger returns in terms of yield and larger output. In this connection, Marxist scholars in general, and Utsa Patnaik [4] in particular, have put forward a supporting thesis by using labour-use index that in a situation of high degree of concentration of the means of production, land owners of hired-labour based holdings operate land in large-scale and demonstrate a shortage of capitalist tendency to produce more with a profit motive. Because, agricultural production does not exclusively depend upon the input of labour per unit of area, but also, investment of capital besides application of better farm technology. These labour-hiring holdings have the ability to retain surplus and indeed possess greater potentials to make investment on new technology, vis-à-vis labour selling households.

It is therefore, argued that these crucial aspects are altogether missed out by the size-class index (extensively used by researchers at different points of time) which does not account for differences in irrigation, soil fertility, capital investments and investible surplus, family size, while arguing that small farms are relatively more efficient than large farms in terms of yield per acre. Therefore, one of the primary purposes of our research (on impact of consolidation of holdings on farm income, yield, employment, new technology etc.) is methodological.

Thus, we propose to use simultaneously two criteria: the size-class index and income group index (not labour-use index used by Utsa Patnaik) in data analysis while the latter takes into the account socio-economic status, investible funds and capability of investment (due to other sources of income, if any) of the farm households in raising its yield, output through application of new/modern farm technology along with development of irrigation.

It is believed that the income group index could genuinely identify and capture farm households better, who have investible surplus and socio-economic status to take advantage of better irrigation, farm mechanization and advanced technology in farming activities vis-à-vis the size-class index.

3.3 Routes for Changes in Agrarian Structure

As a matter of fact, changes in agrarian structure takes place in two ways: first through necessary land legislations directly and their implementation by the governmental agencies and these aggressive policy measures are called land reform measures or institutional changes in agriculture; second, through an indirect method which responds to the spontaneous operation of socio-economic development process. Because, there is a scope for promoting changes in the agrarian structure indirectly through direct influence of such other factors in the social system such as, changes in farm technology, the credit structure, and the extent of non-agricultural employment. Further, implementation of poverty eradication programmes and rural development programmes by the government has a great influence on changes in agrarian structure.

As a result of implementation of these programmes, some sort of development takes place in terms of infrastructural improvement in rural areas and agricultural sector is benefited in variety of ways. For instance, heavy government expenditure on various public work programmes like construction of roads, dams, irrigation projects, power plants etc. leads to tremendous impact and indeed brings a great deal of changes in agrarian structure not only in terms of agricultural improvement, but more importantly, it could increase the level of living through greater food security, and availability of food grains at lower prices at the local level, besides generating huge employment opportunities in the farm sector. Such spontaneous development in agriculture is seen as a part of macro development process of the economy undertaken by the government from time to time.

3.4 Forms of Agrarian Structure Changes

As a consequence of the above changes, land structure also changes in the following three forms such as: (i) changes in ownership on land; (ii) changes in the structure of tenancy (or tenancy reforms); and (iii) changes in the size of operational holdings. Such changes get a fillip, if there is a strong political will. For example, in India, structural changes of land in the form of first and second ones have become possible in the states such as Karnataka, Kerala and West Bengal due to sincere and effective implementation of the land reform measures by the ruling political parties (Leftist/Communist Parties) of the concerned States, besides the very effective role of panchayati raj institutions (PRIs) and gram panchayats (GPs) in particular at the grass roots in the use of ground water potential for irrigation purposes to raise crop yield and food grains production.

In other States, structural changes of land have become slow either due to the discretionary and greater privileges enjoyed by the dominant class or may be due to the non-co-operation/inadequate participation of the lower class/small farmers. But, some structural changes of land in the form of third one, i.e. changes in size of operational holdings has been possible in the states of Punjab, Haryana and Uttar Pradesh due to successful implementation of the scheme of 'consolidation of land holdings' to prevent fragmentation of landholdings, and to increase the size of unit of cultivation for effective utilization of land resources and to facilitate the application of modern farm technology in agriculture. Needless to say, these land reform measures in different forms have a key role in reorganizing the agrarian structure of a country for achieving the ultimate goal of increasing agricultural productivity as well as farm output and in ensuring an egalitarian social structure.

To achieve the twin objectives of economic growth and social equity in a country like India with agrarian base, immediately after its Independence, land reforms were envisaged as important instruments of change directed at removing institutional and motivational obstacles standing in the way of modernization of agriculture and the creation of a more egalitarian social structure. A series of land reform measures like abolition of intermediary in land, tenancy reforms, implementation of ceiling laws and redistribution of ceiling surplus land among landless, co-operative farming, and reorganization of agricultural holdings through the scheme of consolidation of land holdings etc. were enacted both by the

Central and State governments and this was treated as an integral part of the rural development programme in the early post-Independence planning period. These measures were specifically undertaken as basic strategies in the programme for achieving a breakthrough in the custom-oriented and tradition-bound agriculture.

3.5 Fate of Land Reforms

Meanwhile, the issue of land reforms in India and so also in many states either has unconsciously faded away from public mind or been deliberately glossed over the years. Even some veteran economists and academicians have not been reluctant to remark that 'land reform' is now-a-days a dead issue. Many of them are of the opinion that significant achievement has been made in implementation of land reforms. However, despite their claim, it cannot be said that the task of land reforms is quite completed. Land reforms continue to be the critical variable in the solution of the current socio-economic problems in rural areas.

However, the fact remains that the vested interest of the landed elite and their powerful nexus in the political/bureaucratic system has successfully countered to the meaningful land reforms and/or their earnest implementation. The oppressed have either been co-opted with some benefits or further subjugated as the new focus on liberalization, privatization and globalization (LPG) has altered the government priorities and public perceptions.

As a result, we are today at a critical juncture, where land, is more accessed mostly by the urban educated elite, who also happen to be the powerful decision makers in matter for housing, investment, infrastructure building like roads, bridges and setting up massive industries—because, bulk of fertile multi-crop agricultural land, waste land and forest land is being diverted for the above purposes. This is evident from the recent incidents of unrest and protest by common people at 'Kalinga Nagar' area of Jajpur District, at Paradeep of Kendrapada District of Odisha and at Nandigram in East

Medinipur district and Singur area in Hooghly district of West Bengal against the acquisition of farm land by government for setting up of industries by private industrialists like Tatas, Posco of South Korea, Salim Group Company of Indonesia etc. and the resultant dislocation of people.

Thus, the above factors have caused a decline in the operated/cultivated area and have quietly threatened food security. In the bargain, the existence of land as a basis of livelihood—for subsistence, survival, social justice and human dignity—has largely been missed out. In this respect, little has been addressed in the policy perspective under the existing land reform measures.

Similarly, nothing tangible has been done to improve agricultural production and ameliorate the conditions of the poorest of the poor. This is evident from the present rural socio-economic scenario and the existing agricultural situation in the state. If the land structure includes vast numbers of small and fragmented farms, it poses serious impediments to rational allocation of land and agricultural productivity and nullifies the objective of achieving economic growth.

Likewise, when land is used as a tool in the hands of a few to hijack country's economic independence and also State's food security and livelihood and subvert its social processes, then the efforts to achieve the objective of social equity may be annulled. To achieve the twin objectives of economic growth and social equity in a country like India, land reforms should be looked from the view point of an 'ideology' rather than a mere 'programme' of action. Further, it should be reflected at the level of formulation of economic programmes as well as at the level of their implementation.

3.6 Food Security Concerns

Consequent upon massive industrialization and urbanization, in the recent years, it has begun to pose threats to food security very quietly and may endanger it in future. In an agrarian economy, when more land goes out of agricultural sector for non-agricultural purposes, production of food grains and, in some cases, land productivity are likely to cause dismal performance. This loss in agricultural sector can only be compensated by augmenting agricultural productivity and output through a very progressive land reform measure, such as consolidation of land holdings, which paves the ways for adoption of modern farm technology, optimal use of available irrigation water, options towards alternative sources of irrigation, crop diversification, higher cropping intensity, use of modern farm inputs and farm mechanization etc.

Sub-division of holdings indicates the diminution of the total size of the individual farm holding into small and uneconomic holdings, as a result of among other causes, partition of property between different heirs under the laws of succession or inheritance. With the rapid growth of population, there is a continuous pressure on land, which results in sub-division and fragmentation of holdings into minute strips and tiny size of the unit of cultivation. These uneconomic units of cultivation are not viable for modern cultivation with new technology. Such sub-division and fragmentation of holdings is a major cause for the low productivity in agriculture and pose serious threats to the food security of the small land holders.

There is no doubt regarding many disadvantages resulting from the fragmentation of holdings. The small and fragmented landholdings delineate the peculiar features such as imbalance in the land-man ratio, excess labour requirement, higher cost of cultivation per unit of land, inferior farm practices, difficulty in irrigation and soil conservation practices, difficulty in weed and pest control, low productivity per unit of land holding (ASCI Report, 2000). [5] The main disadvantages of fragmentation and sub-division of holdings are as under:

1. Full and proper land utilization becomes impossible and often, the small size of holdings is considered unprofitable to cultivate.
2. It counters to effective land utilization since improved

agricultural practices cannot be adopted.

3. A good deal of time, energy, and expenditure of the farmer is wasted in moving labour, cattle/bullocks, seed, manure and irrigation water from one plot to another and in bringing the harvested crop to a single threshing floor (Randhawa, 1974). [6]
4. Supervision of farm operation becomes difficult.
5. Expenses on irrigation, farming, drainage etc. continue to increase.
6. Sinking of a tube well or use of canal irrigation is practically impossible on scattered holdings, even if, sufficient water is available.
7. Fragmentation brings in a great deal of disputes regarding boundaries, field channels, leading farmers into expensive litigation against each other. Thus, access to the scattered plots becomes difficult during crop season and leads to disputes and tensions over trespass etc.
8. Fragmentation of land holdings results in loss of land on boundaries, hedges, drainages, fencing and path ways etc.
9. It debars tractor cultivation and the use of modern machines and labour saving devices in agriculture.
10. Sub-division of land progressively reduces the average size of holdings and raises variable costs on seed, manure, fencing etc., and hence, it entails capital duplication.

Thus, fragmented and small uneconomic holdings are non-viable units for cultivation. Precisely, all these in consolidated form brings about progressive agricultural deterioration, lower productivity and continued food insecurity for small farm holders, lower income of the farming community, thereby increasing the poverty of masses in the rural areas.

3.7 Consolidation of Land Holdings

Despite some disadvantages, consolidation of land holdings as a progressive land reform measure is designed to reverse the division of land into small units. Legislation on consolidation of land holdings is one of the important measures of land reforms in India. The legislative measures on consolidation consist of two parts. One relates to prevention of fragmentation and the second, deals with the procedures for administration of the scheme of consolidation of holdings. It is believed that consolidation of land holdings could be an effective instrument in the concerted efforts aimed at making agriculture in a region more competitive and also in promoting rural development. In India, consolidation of fragmented agricultural land holdings has been made an integral part of the land reform measures in the early post-Independence planning period. Historically, the policy on consolidation of land holdings was conceptualized in the Second Five Year Plan. Since then, successive Five Year Plans have accordingly been laying stress on the implementation of the scheme of consolidation of fragmented land holdings for planned development of villages, and increased agricultural output.

However, it was believed that the scheme of consolidation of holdings could enhance farm output, productivity, through a better cropping pattern, use of better farm technology including irrigation facilities that could ensure food security to small land holders on sustainable basis and raise their level of living. Besides, consolidation could also be used to improve the land tenure in support of rural development by addressing the issue of land fragmentation. It can be an effective instrument in formulating strategies and projects that could enhance the quality of rural life by improving natural resource management, environmental conservation, providing infrastructure and services, creating employment opportunities to vast rural labour force and ameliorating socio-economic conditions of the rural small land holders.

Therefore, consolidation of holdings is not merely a re-arrangement or exchange of plots but it could be an effective instrument in rural development to bring out a great deal of socio-economic gains. This is because the scheme provides ample opportunity for re-planning and reconstructing the village economy, infrastructure and the society in the countryside by making provision of inter-village roads and reserving land for public utilities such as schools, play-grounds, dispensaries, grazing fields, tanks etc.

Consolidation of land holdings can also assist farmers to amalgamate their fragmented small holdings at one place and facilitate the creation of competitive agricultural production arrangements by enabling farmers to have farms with fewer parcels that are larger and better shaped through expansion of the size of their holdings. For example, a farmer who owns one hectare of land being divided into five parcels scattered at different places may increasingly benefit from a consolidation scheme which results in a single block having equal value. Although the holding size remains the same, a larger and better shaped parcel after consolidation may allow the farmer to introduce better farming techniques.

Besides, land consolidation projects may result in substantial changes in land tenure arrangements and these actions are executed under the leadership of a State. Nonetheless, land consolidation is not a form of expropriation. This Scheme is not at all meant to dispossess people from their rights over land. This does not in any way make people landless. Instead, it enables all land owners to enjoy benefits of consolidation and enhance their capabilities. Therefore, active participation of farmers and other rural residents in the process is essential to make the scheme a success on sustainable basis.

End Notes

1. Bharadwaj, Krishna (1974), 'Production Conditions in Indian Agriculture: A Study Based on Farm Management Surveys', Cambridge University Press, Bentley House, London.
2. Mallik, R.M. (1994), 'Economic Structure and Farm Viability', Commonwealth Publishers, New Delhi.
3. Sen, Amartya Kumar (1962), 'An Aspect of Indian Agriculture', Economic Weekly, Vol. 14 (A.N.), February.
4. Patnaik, Utsa (1972), 'Capitalist Development in Agriculture, Oxford.
5. Administrative Staff College of India Report, Hyderabad (2000), '*Study on Review of Performance of Schemes of Consolidation*

of Land Holdings and Computerization of Land Records' submitted to the Ministry of Rural Development, Government of India, New Delhi.

6. Ranndhwa, M.S. (1947-1981), *'A History of Agriculture in India'*, ICAR, New Delhi, Vol. XIV, Chapter 3, p. 27.

4

Land Reforms: Constituents and Critical Appraisal

Agrarian reforms have been a core issue for rural reconstruction as a means of ensuring social justice to actual tillers and the landless rural poor, thereby creating a sustainable base for the overall growth of the industrial and tertiary sectors of our economy. Generating greater access of landless rural poor to land is considered an important component of the effort aimed at poverty alleviation.

In India, land is the prime resource of the vast majority of the poor deriving livelihood from agriculture. The pattern of land ownership inherited from the colonial rulers was, and continues to be, unjust and exploitative. A fair distribution of land resources is a pre-requisite for agricultural development and social justice. Ever since Independence, land reforms have been recognised as a crucial element of the poverty removal strategy and for modernisation of agriculture.

The use of improved farm technology and inputs depends upon a conducive institutional framework. The objective of land reforms is to revamp the institutional framework by redistributing land in favour of the poor, providing security of tenure, regulating rents on land, and consolidating small and fragmented holdings.

Underlining the need for land reforms, the First Five Year Plan (1951-56) observed, "The future of land ownership and cultivation constitutes perhaps the most fundamental issue in national development. To a large extent the pattern of economic and social organisation will depend upon the manner in which the land problem is resolved. Sooner or later, the principles and objectives of policy for land cannot but influence policy in other sectors as well". [1]

4.1 Constituents of Land Reforms

Broadly speaking, land reforms constitute the following:

1. Abolition of intermediaries.
2. Tenancy reforms including security of tenure, regulation of rent, and conferment of ownership rights on tenants.
3. Ceiling on land holdings and distribution of surplus land among landless workers and marginal farmers.
4. Consolidation of holdings.
5. Protection of tribals' rights in land.
6. Modernization of land administration.

4.1.1 Abolition of Intermediaries: The British created the *zamindari* system with two objectives in mind: (a) to increase the revenue for the East India Company, and (b) to create a loyal class for themselves in an otherwise hostile alien country. However, the *zamindari* system was very exploitative and proved a drag on the development of agriculture.

Soon after Independence, various State Governments enacted laws to abolish the *zamindari* system and establish direct relationship between the tiller of the soil and the government. The abolition of intermediary rights has been the major achievement in the field of land reform. In varying degrees these rights had a long history behind them and they were the essential elements of power in the feudal structure. As a result of the elimination of these rights, in States which had zamindari, jagirdari or other similar tenures, the State has now come into direct contact with the occupier of the land.

4.1.2 Tenancy Reforms: Tenancy legislations were introduced after independence to confer ownership on the tenant and some measure of security of tenure, coupled with rent regulation to prevent exploitation of tenants and increase agricultural productivity in such farms.

Although agricultural tenancies are banned in most States, the incidence of some type of tenancy, particularly in various forms of crop sharing, is still substantial in some regions. As tenancy is contracted orally, and in most cases in violation of law, the tiller's position is precarious and he has no incentive to cultivate land efficiently. In several regions, the existing provisions lead landowners to keep the land fallow for fear of losing their rights. It also restricts poor peoples' access to land through leasing in. Experience has shown that measures to ban tenancy are not usually effective and large amount of oral/concealed tenancy continues to exist among all categories of rural households. Thus decrease in lease market participation with economic growth indicates that tenancy restrictions are constraining the supply of land in the rental market.

In the Indian agrarian structure, intermediaries cannot be abolished altogether. In other words, a total ban on leasing or sub-leasing of land is neither feasible nor desirable. A minor, a widow, a mentally retarded person, or a member of the armed forces may have to lease out land to others. Thus, considerable land is held under tenancy and sub-tenancy in different parts of the country. It is, however, necessary to minimise the malpractices associated with letting and sub-letting of land. Tenancy legislations should be framed in a manner which balances the interest of the landowner and the tenant and improves access to land, its utilization and releases the forces of production leading to improved agricultural productivity.

A. Security of Tenure: Security of tenure is necessary for producers to have the incentive for investment for productivity. Land tenure security should signify that legitimately held land use rights are not disturbed without legitimate cause and without due process, and any such contested rights shall be resolved by an appropriate dispute settlement mechanism.

Tenants in the agricultural sector are ordinarily categorised into three groups: (a) occupancy or permanent tenants, (b) tenants-at-will, and (c) sub-tenants. The rights of the occupancy tenants are safe and they do not fear eviction so long as they pay rent on time. However, tenants-at-will and sub-tenants are in a weak position and their existence depends on the mercy of the landlords. Laws have been passed in most of the States to protect tenants from ejection. According to these laws, land may be resumed by the owner for personal cultivation. It is interesting to note that in many cases landlords force the tenants to *voluntarily surrender* the land to circumvent the law. The so-called *voluntary surrenders* are in fact the result of pressures and threats.

B. Regulation of Rents: During British rule, *zamindars* charged high rents from the tenants. Soon after Independence, laws were enacted by the States to regulate the limit of rents with a view to reduce the burden on the tenants. Broadly speaking, rents have been fixed at one-fourth or one-fifth of the total produce. Unfortunately, laws fixing maximum limit of rent have not been effective. This is due to the fact that the position of tenants' vis-à-vis landlords is weak. In most cases, the illiterate tenants are not aware of the law and even if they know about it, they are unable to assert their rights.

C. Ownership Rights: Legislative provisions have been made in many States, providing for conferment of ownership rights on tenants or for allowing cultivating tenants to acquire ownership rights on payment of a reasonable compensation to the land-owners. Some States have acquired ownership of land from the land-owners and have transferred them to the tenants who have to pay a certain amount or premium to the State.

The Government has repeatedly advocated that tenants should be made the owners of land they cultivate. However, the tenants have not been able to exercise their right to purchase ownership of land cultivated by them. This is partly due to the inability of the tenants to pay the purchase price and also due to the fear of antagonising the landlords.

4.1.3 Ceiling on Land Holdings: An important aspect of land reforms relates to the ceiling on land holdings. A ceiling on holdings means fixing statutory maximum limit on the amount of land which an individual or a family can hold. The surplus land so obtained is distributed among landless workers and marginal farmers. The case for imposition of land ceiling rests on socio-economic grounds. It aims at improving the economic status of the rural poor. Since land is the main source of income in rural areas, it should be equitably distributed.

Critics of land ceiling have argued that such a policy leads to break-up of big farms and hence decline in productivity. However, studies based on farm management data have revealed that farm size is not significant in securing high yields.

A. Main Features of Land Ceiling Laws: Since agriculture is a State subject in India therefore different laws pertaining to ceiling on holdings operate in different parts of the country. Laws on imposition of ceiling on agricultural holdings were enacted by several States during the 1950s and 1960s. These were implemented with varying degrees of effectiveness in different States. Broadly speaking, the following common points are noticeable in the ceiling laws of various States.

1. Ceiling laws have normally exempted the following categories of land: (a) tea, coffee, and rubber plantations, (b) orchards, (c) cattle breeding, dairying, wool raising farms, (d) land held by industrial and commercial undertakings, and (e) land belonging to religious and charitable institutions.
2. 1972 National Guidelines recommended ceiling limits ranging from 10-18 acres for irrigated land with two crops, 27 acres for irrigated land with one crop and 54 acres for dry land.
3. Unit of application is generally the family of five members: husband, wife and three minor children. Some States have adopted individual ownership as the unit of application.
4. In the distribution of surplus land, priority has been accorded to landless agricultural workers and marginal farmers.
5. Compensation has been fixed in multiples of land revenue payable for the land.
6. Most of these laws have been placed in the Ninth Schedule

of the Constitution so that they are not challenged in courts of law on grounds of infringement of fundamental rights.

B. Problems Associated with Imposition of Ceiling: The imposition of ceiling on land holdings is a ticklish problem. First of all, land is not alike in the whole of India or even within a State. Therefore, different ceiling limits have to be fixed on the basis of quality of land and the nature of agricultural operations. Secondly, the unit of application has to be decided, i.e. whether ceiling would apply to holdings of an individual or family. Thirdly, what exemptions, if any, would be made. Fourthly, how the persons affected by ceiling would be compensated and how the surplus land would be allotted.

C. Failure of Ceiling Laws: Although based on sound social philosophy, land ceiling policy has not delivered the goods. Big landlords have successfully circumvented the laws by various ingenious devices. They have resorted to malafide transfers of land, viz. transfers among the family members, *benami* transfers, and concealment of ownership. The bureaucracy and the judiciary have also not been helpful in the implementation of ceiling legislations. Expressing dissatisfaction about the implementation of ceiling laws, the Eleventh Five Year Plan (2007-12) remarked, "The quantum of land declared surplus is far short of land which was estimated to be surplus on the basis of various national surveys. Thus, it is clear that reform measures have not been able to achieve the desired impact. The total area declared surplus so far has been 73.5 lakh acres only, of which 53.9 lakh acres have been distributed. The distribution of the remaining area of land declared surplus is held up mainly due to litigation.

There are also widespread complaints that lands allotted to the rural poor under the ceiling laws are not in their possession. In some cases, it has also been alleged that pattas were issued to the beneficiaries but possession was not delivered in respect of the lands shown in the pattas or corresponding changes in the records of rights were not made. It has also been the experience that rural poor allottees of ceiling surplus land are dragged into litigation by the erstwhile land-owners and against which the allottees are unable to defend themselves. Besides, a number of benami and clandestine transactions have resulted in illegal possession of significant amounts of lands above ceiling limits. For all these reasons the results of implementation of the ceiling laws are far from satisfactory". [2]

D. Distribution of Bhoodan Land and Government Wastelands: The Bhoodan movement has been a part of the social movement for equitable distribution of land through peoples' processes. In some States the movement met with considerable success. Distribution of Government wastelands has been one of the key strategies of land reforms in the country. It has been the accepted policy of the Central Government that wastelands at the disposal of the State Governments should be distributed amongst eligible rural poor. The criteria governing the distribution of ceiling surplus land should also apply to the distribution of wasteland.

4.1.4 Consolidation of Holdings: A disturbing feature of the Indian agrarian scene is the declining size of holdings. As a result of population explosion and rural indebtedness, holdings are becoming smaller and fragmented. Therefore, consolidation of holdings is an integral part of land reforms in India. Consolidation can be either voluntary or compulsory.

Successive Five Year Plans have been laying stress on consolidation of fragmented land holdings for planned development of villages and increased agricultural output. Consequently, many States had enacted legislations and had taken up the work relating to consolidation of land holdings. Laws regarding consolidation of holdings differ from State to State. The States of Uttar Pradesh, Haryana and Punjab have achieved commendable success. In the State of Uttar Pradesh, even now, consolidation of land holdings is in operation. In other States, work was continued for some years but lost momentum thereafter.

Various factors have worked against consolidation.

1. Fear of displacement among tenants and share-croppers.

2. Advantage of having land in fragmented parcels in the event of floods and other natural calamities.
3. Apprehensions that the bigger farmers would get a better deal.

4.1.5 Protection of Tribals' Rights in Land: Land is the major tangible productive asset that members of scheduled tribes possess. Tribals also have very strong emotional attachment to their land. Some of the social practices and religious rituals of tribals are also connected with land, which occupies a pivotal place in their psyche. An important fact is that community ownership of tribal land continues to be the dominant mode in tribal societies and takes precedence over individual ownership. The increase in extremist activities in many tribal districts can be linked to issues related to land including alienation of tribal land.

Article 46 of the Constitution enjoins upon the States the obligation to promote the interests of Scheduled Castes and Scheduled Tribes and to protect them from social injustice and all forms of exploitation. The State Governments have accepted the policy of prohibiting the transfer of land from tribals to non-tribals and for restoration of alienated tribal lands to them. The States with large tribal population have since enacted laws for this purpose.

The enactment of the Scheduled Tribes and other Traditional Dwellers (Recognition of Forest Rights) Act, 2006, and rules framed under it, will provide the much needed protection from exploitation of tribals. The legislation, which was notified for operation with effect from December 31, 2007, has been widely welcomed by scheduled tribes and other traditional forest dwellers who now have legal rights on forest land which they have been cultivating or using over generations for eking out their livelihood.

4.1.6 Modernization of Land Administration: Land administration in India is plagued by many infirmities. Ambiguous titles, informal tenancy arrangements and other related problems have not only affected productivity of agriculture, they have also forced migration of people, both landless and marginal farmers in search of employment to urban areas as well as of the landed gentry, giving rise to absentee landlordism, who do not lease out land for fear of loosing the land titles. Hence, an efficient and corruption free land administration, coupled with a dynamically adaptive land policy, has a vital role in increasing agriculture growth and poverty reduction. Accurate and updated land records are crucial for the security of land rights, reduction in disputes and conflicts, lower transaction costs and corruption, and implementation of land reforms.

A. Computerization of Land Records (CLR): The Centrally-sponsored scheme on Computerisation of Land Records (CLR) was started in 1988-89 with 100 percent Central assistance by taking up a pilot project in one District each of 8 States, viz. Rangareddy (A.P.), Sonitpur (Assam), Singhbhum (Bihar), Gandhinagar (Gujarat), Morena (M.P.), Wardha (Maharashtra), Mayurbhanj (Odisha) and Dungarpur (Rajasthan) to remove the problems inherent in the manual systems of maintenance and updating of land records and to meet the requirements of various groups of users. It was decided that efforts should be made to computerise 'Core Data' contained in land records, to assist development planning and to make records accessible to people/planners and administrators.

The main objectives of the scheme are:

1. Ensuring that landowners get computerized copies of ownership, crop and tenancy and updated copies of records of rights (RoRs) on demand.
2. Realizing low-cost and easily-reproducible basic land record data through reliable and durable preservation of old records.
3. Ensuring accuracy, transparency and speedy dispute resolution.
4. Facilitating fast and efficient retrieval of information for decision-making.

5. According legal sanctity to computer-generated certificates of land records after authentication by the authorized revenue official.
6. Setting up a comprehensive land information system for better land-based planning and utilization of land resources.
7. Focusing on citizen-centric services related to land and revenue information.

Under the CLR scheme, 100 percent financial assistance is provided to States and UTs for completing data entry work, setting up computer centres at the tehsil or taluk or block or circle level, sub-divisional level, district level and a monitoring cell at the State level. Funds are also provided for imparting training on computer awareness and applications software to revenue officials for regular updating of records of rights and smooth operation of computer centres. Digitization of maps has also been allowed under the CLR scheme.

Initially, it was decided that basic infrastructure would be created at the district level for undertaking data entry. After completion of data entry (including verification and validation at the district level), data has to be ported to tehsil or taluk computer centres for regular operation.

Therefore, in 1997-98, it was decided to extend the scheme to the tehsil or taluk level to facilitate better accessibility to computerized copies of RoRs for landowners.

The phased coverage of the scheme is given below:

1. During the Seventh Plan, funds were sanctioned for taking up the programme in 24 districts;
2. During the Eighth Plan, funds were sanctioned for taking up the programme in additional 299 districts;
3. During the Ninth Plan, funds were sanctioned for taking up the programme in additional 259 districts;
4. In 1997-98, it was decided that the scheme be extended to the taluk or tehsil or block level to facilitate distribution on demand of computerized copies of RoRs from the tehsil or taluk computer centre. Accordingly, in the Ninth Plan

period, funds were sanctioned for setting up computer centres at 2787 tehsils or taluks;

5. During the Tenth Plan period, the scheme has been extended to cover 1,615 more tehsils/taluks/blocks/anchals/circles, setting up of computer centres in 1,019 sub-divisions, land records data centres in 365 districts and monitoring cell at 16 State Headquarters.

B. Strengthening of Revenue Administration and Updating of Land Records (SRA&ULR): The importance of land records in the rural areas cannot be over-emphasised. The causes of rural conflicts have often been traced to improper maintenance of land records. Updation is vital for systematic maintenance of land records to reflect ground realities in sync with ownership changes, ensure genuine land transactions and implement rural development programmes for effective enforcement of land reforms. It will minimize land disputes and create social harmony in villages.

Although the importance of a proper land records system has been emphasized from the First Five Year Plan, land records in most parts of the country are not in good shape largely due to resource constraints. As per existing instructions, records of rights are prepared by carrying out cadastral surveys followed by settlement operations; these are time consuming, call for huge staff and are expensive. Equipment used in these operations is also outdated. Even where there is a system of periodical updating of land records, lack of adequate revenue machinery and proper infrastructure and absence of training are responsible for poorly maintained land records.

With a view to assisting the States/UTs in the task of updating of Land Records, a Centrally-sponsored scheme of Strengthening of Revenue Administration and Updating of Land Records (SRA&ULR) was started in 1987-88 on a 50:50 sharing basis between the Centre and the States. Union Territories are provided 100 percent Central assistance.

The main objectives of the scheme are:

1. Strengthening of survey and settlement organizations in

the States/UTs for early completion of the survey and settlement operations and preparation of land records in areas where this work still remains to be done.

2. Setting up of survey and settlement institutions especially in the North Eastern Region, where survey and settlement operations are yet to be done and land records introduced.
3. Imparting pre-service and in-service training to revenue, survey and settlement staff and strengthening of training infrastructure for this purpose. Providing facilities for modernisation of survey and settlement operations, printing of survey maps, reports/documents, storage, copying and updating of land and crop records using, among other things, latest science and technology inputs.
4. Strengthening of revenue machinery at village and immediate supervisory levels on a selective basis to make the workload of these functionaries manageable.

Under this scheme financial assistance has been provided to States/UTs for purchase of modern survey equipments like global positioning system (GPS), EDM, total stations, theodolites, work stations, aerial surveys, office equipments like photocopiers, laminating machines, binding machines and basic facilities to improve work efficiency at the lower levels of revenue administration, construction of record rooms for proper storage of land records, office-cum-residence of *patwaries*, construction/repair/renovation of survey and settlement training institutes and equipments for training etc. The scheme has been in operation in all the States/UTs.

C. National Land Records Modernization Programme (NLRMP): It has been proposed to merge the two Centrally-sponsored schemes, namely, Computerisation of Land Records (CLR) and Strengthening of Revenue Administration and Updating of Land Records (SRA&ULR) in the shape of the National Land Records Modernization Programme (NLRMP). The NLRMP has been conceptualized as a major systems reforms initiative that is concerned not merely with computerization, updating and maintenance of land records and validation of titles, but also as a program that will add value and provide a comprehensive tool for development planning wherever location-specific information is required. Three layers of data: (a) spatial data from satellite imagery/aerial photography, (b) topographic maps and other data from the Survey of India and Forest Survey of India, and (c) land records data—both records of rights (RoRs) and maps will be integrated and harmonized on a geographic information system (GIS) platform.

The primary focus of the programme will be on: (i) providing citizen services, such as providing records of rights (RoRs) with maps to scale; other land-based certificates such as caste certificates, income certificates (particularly in rural areas), domicile certificates; information for eligibility for development programmes; land passbooks, etc., and (ii) developing a comprehensive tool for supporting and planning developmental, regulatory, and disaster management activities, wherever land-based information is required.

In the context of modernization of management of land records and titles, the Eleventh Five Year Plan (2007-12) observed, "Two Centrally Sponsored Schemes (CSS) currently under implementation are the computerisation of land records and strengthening of revenue administration.

These would be subsumed in the proposed National Land Records Management Programme, which would be launched shortly as a pilot project in one district in each State. After the validation of the proof of concept within the next two years, the scheme would be extended to the entire country. It is expected that digitisation of land records after undertaking comprehensive land survey would be completed by the end of Twelfth Plan period. It is expected that after availability of this basic record, the country could move towards the 'Torrens' system in the Thirteenth Five Year Plan." [3]

4.2 Recent Five Year Plans on Land Reforms

4.2.1 Eighth Five Year Plan (1992-97): Eighth Plan regarded landlessness as the root cause of rural poverty. It, therefore, stressed the urgency to speed up land reforms. To quote, "In a country where agriculture is the principal means of livelihood, access to land is a major source of employment and income. This access could be achieved in two ways either by a more equitable redistribution of land or by providing security of tenure to tenants and share-croppers who are the actual cultivators. The scope with respect to redistribution is limited. After the imposition of the ceilings, 7.23 million acres of land was declared surplus of which 4.65 million acres had been distributed by the end of the Seventh Plan. Of the remaining, a large proportion is under litigation. With the average size of holdings declining, there is no possibility of fresh ceilings. Hence, efforts will have to be made to detect the surplus land hitherto unavailable, to distribute the existing surplus expeditiously and ensure that allotees retain possession of land." [4]

4.2.2 Ninth Five Year Plan (1997-02): Regretting on the poor progress of land reforms in the post-Independence period, the Ninth Plan remarked, "Despite attempts at land reforms over successive Plan periods, the basic character of the agrarian economy has not undergone any structural change. The pattern of land distribution is highly skewed, with a high concentration of land in the hands of a few land owners on the one hand and the growing number of marginal and sub-marginal farmers on the other." [5] Noting another disquieting trend in the context of land reforms, the Plan further regretted, "In the wake of the economic liberalisation in certain States like Karnataka, the industry and the large farmers are being given exemption from ceiling laws without seeking the permission of the Government of India. This would certainly go against the interest of the poor as it would increase landlessness and depress agricultural wages. Hence, this issue requires close examination, before such exemptions are given." [6]

4.2.3 Tenth Five Year Plan (2002-07): Lauding the achievements of land reforms after Independence, the Tenth

Plan observed, "Successive Five Year Plans have addressed the issue of secure rights in land for increased agricultural productivity under the land reforms programme. Land reform legislations, besides abolishing intermediaries and providing ownership rights to farmers, also provided for security of tenure to tenants and regulation of rent. Actual cultivators were brought into a direct relationship with the State. The abolition of intermediaries succeeded in providing ownership rights to a large number of tenants. The advent of the *green revolution* technology coupled with schemes of asset transfer under IRDP has contributed significantly to the increased incomes not only from agricultural operations but also on account of diversification into animal husbandry. [7]

4.2.4 Eleventh Five Year Plan (2007-12): The Approach Paper on the Eleventh Plan released by the Government in November 2006 while underlining the role of land relations on agricultural productivity remarked, "Land relations can have a major impact on agricultural productivity and production. Inequality in land distribution and insecurity of tenure etc., are often at the bottom of many forms of social discrimination and domination based on gender, caste, minority and tribal affiliations. The National Commission on Farmers has placed the unfinished agenda in land reform first in its list of five factors central to the present agrarian crisis, and states "the first and foremost task of the National Policy for Farmers should be in the area of land reform with particular reference to tenancy laws, distribution of ceiling surplus land, attention to common property and wasteland resources and the consolidation of holdings. Following the conferment of land rights to women under the Hindu Succession Amendment Act (2005), the provision of appropriate support services to women farmers has become urgent. Joint *Pattas* are essential for women to get access to credit. Also, there should be stringent restrictions on the diversion of prime farmland for non-farm purposes.

Since migration and feminisation are increasing trends,

land reforms that make tenancy legal and give well defined rights to tenants and to women are now more necessary than ever, not only to reduce distress but also to increase agricultural growth. Facilitating leasing of land for cultivation is necessary to prevent cultivated land from turning fallow due to migration of owners to urban areas. Lack of recognised tenancy rights makes it difficult for *de facto* tenants to get credit from formal sources. Tenants without legal rights do not have proper incentive to develop the land and this explains part of the yield gap. Similarly, a woman without property title is unable to get credit when the male member is away. Giving access to land and homesteads to those lacking these is effective in reducing poverty and this still remains the most powerful way to bring dignity in the lives of today's excluded. This, along with the more general need to record land titles properly where these are weak, is also one way to deal effectively with encroachment and non-participation that plague watershed and wasteland development programmes. With EGA in place, such programmes can be stepped up very substantially to address natural resource regeneration but the incentive issues related to land will have to be addressed". [8]

4.3 Critical Appraisal of Land Reforms in India

Soon after Independence, land reform programme was started with great fanfare to bring social justice to the rural masses. Legislations were enacted in different States for the abolition of *zamindari* system, fixing ceiling on land holdings, regulation of rents, and security of tenure. Although the policy of land reforms was a step in the right direction, it failed to achieve the desired results. The experience so far has been disappointing. Various factors have worked against the success of land reforms.

4.3.1 Lack of Political Will: Agriculture being a State subject, different laws have been passed at different times by the State Governments. In many cases, States have flouted the guidelines provided by the Central Government. Since State legislatures are dominated by the big landlords, there is often a gap between the policy and the actual legislation. Loopholes in the legislations and lukewarm attitude in implementing legal provisions reflect lack of political will.

4.3.2 Indifferent Attitude of Bureaucracy: Laws enacted by State legislatures have not been implemented sincerely by the administrative wing of the Governments. It is observed that many of the bureaucrats and functionaries at the State, district and the village level are themselves landlords of varying status. It is unlikely that they will co-operate in the implementation of land reforms laws.

4.3.3 Legal System Protecting Right to Property: In their bid to resist land reforms, the vested interests in land have frequently resorted to litigation. Unfortunately, the judiciary has often protected the landlords in the name of sanctity of private property. For example, the Supreme Court has ruled that compensation relating to land ceiling laws should be given at market value. In 1974, Parliament passed unanimously the 34th amendment to 9th Schedule of the Constitution thereby taking the land ceiling laws away from judicial review. However, the problem has not been solved by the inclusion of these laws in the 9th Schedule. These laws have been challenged on other grounds such as inconsistency with Article 14 (equality before law).

4.3.4 Absence of Pressure from Rural Poor: Landless workers and marginal farmers, prospective beneficiaries of land reforms, are unorganised, inarticulate and submissive. The lack of pressure from their side has weakened the enthusiasm of those interested in land reforms. *The Report of the Task Force on Agrarian Relations* (1973) had suggested the organisation of the poor peasantry into strong trade unions.

4.3.5 Absence of Up-to-date Land Records: In the absence of up-to-date land records, excessive litigation and delays in courts have taken place. Compilation and updating of land records is a pre-requisite for the successful implementation of land laws.

In short, land reforms have moved at a snail's speed, if not totally failed.

End Notes

1. Government of India, Planning Commission, *First Five Year Plan* (1951-56), p. 184.
2. Government of India, Planning Commission, *Eleventh Five Year Plan* (2007-12), Volume III, pp. 29-30.
3. Ibid, p. 29.
4. Government of India, Planning Commission, *Eighth Five Year Plan* (1992-97), Volume I, p. 13.
5. Government of India, Planning Commission, *Ninth Five Year Plan* (1997-2002), Volume II, p. 24.
6. Ibid, p. 37.
7. Government of India, Planning Commission, *Tenth Five Year Plan* (2002-07), Volume II, p. 307.
8. Government of India, Planning Commission, *An Approach to Eleventh Five Year Plan*, November 2006, pp. 30-31.

5

Consolidation of Land Holdings: Review of Literature

Many research studies have made observations on the changed scenario in farming due to the positive effects of consolidation of holdings on farm production, productivity and farm income. The review of literature is based on the following:

1. Reaction of people to consolidation proceedings.
2. Short-term effects of consolidation of holdings.
3. Long-term effects of consolidation of holdings.

5.1 Reaction of People to Consolidation Proceedings

There are studies focusing on the attitudes of villagers towards consolidation and their immediate reaction to consolidation proceedings and the problems and deficiencies, which create obstacles in the progress of implementation of the scheme of consolidation of land holdings. Among them, the important studies are by Kaushik (1953); Elder (1962); Rizvi (1965) and others. In this connection, villagers' reaction to consolidation proceedings is one dimension relating to the general shift in the attitude of the villagers from suspicion and resentment to broad acceptance of such a reform measure in land.

Kaushik's (1953) [1] study is intended to bring to light certain basic difficulties and bottlenecks involved in the implementation of the consolidation scheme. These are: (i) discouraging attitude of the land owners to accept the Consolidation Scheme and their reluctance to part with their lands for exchange because of their emotional and sentimental attachment to their ancestral landed property; (ii) in many cases record of rights of the land owners are not available and properly maintained, most of the land records are not updated, which need to be corrected for proper valuation; (iii) adequate number of implementing staff and personnel need to be employed and they need to be properly trained and educated on the scheme as the work is technical in nature; (iv) financial problems mount in the process of the implementation of the scheme; (v) lack of co-operation by the landlords and the rumour spread against the scheme by a group of hostile people; (vi) there is a strong feeling amongst the farmers that consolidation may not secure concurrence of the farmers as most of the farmers did not co-operate. Kaushik emphasizes on farmers' participation, and their concurrence in the implementation of the scheme so as to make the programme a success.

However, the policy suggestions of Kaushik are not quite sufficient to motivate and build confidence among the farming communities. The need of a strong political will and the creation of awareness with active role of the State besides some elements of compulsion have to be highlighted and emphasized for the success of the programme. These aspects are however ignored by Kaushik in his study.

Elder (1962) [2] examined the reactions of villagers to consolidation in Husanipur district of Uttar Pradesh (approximately two hundred miles west of Lucknow), in 1958 and 1961. Initially, Elder found widespread hostility towards consolidation efforts and a high degree of suspicion on the part of the villagers. When he visited the area again three and a half year later, the same farmers expressed much different and opposite views on the utility of consolidation. The villagers claimed that consolidation has 'streamlined' the farming methods by reorganizing land into compact blocks, and it has facilitated the expansion of well irrigation. This appeared to be a positive impact of consolidation of land through exploitation of ground water potential in the village unexplored till then.

Rizvi, Sabzwari and Sharif (1965) [3] examined the process of consolidation of agricultural holdings in selected villages of Peshawar district of Pakistan through intensive field investigation. Their study reveals the adverse attitudes of the land owners towards consolidation scheme and also the factors which have impeded its progress. Their objective was to bring to the surface the difficulties and dangers of the programme, (if any), especially involved in the implementation of the scheme. However, the study throws some light on the attitude of owners as well as of the staff of the department towards consolidation of holdings. Though the pattern of ownership varies from village to village and even within the village itself, the study shows that large and medium sized owners (mostly non-cultivating owners), and also very small owners (having average holding 0.4 acres as in village Banda Sheikh Ismail) are more favourably inclined towards consolidation.

However, the small owners (having average holdings 2.3 acres in Ali Beg and 2 acres in village Haji Pando) who are the actual tillers of land, could not be convinced of the benefits of the scheme and therefore, opposed the consolidation proceeding. Since the consolidation department has not tried to gain their confidence and is unable to convince them regarding the likely positive social and economic benefits, the small owners not only refuse to accept the scheme, but also, deny the benefits of consolidation of holdings.

The authors point out that the department grossly fails to inspire, motivate the people and therefore, create more bitterness than goodwill. Thus, the slow progress of consolidation is an eloquent testimony to the failure of a right approach for achieving the desired results. Instead, the people should have been asked to exercise their rights to know about the merits of the scheme, the authors point out. Rizvi and his colleagues, however, rightly suggest that all development programmes, unless preceded by a proper educational programme, might enter to the rocks of uncertainty and might result in wastage of limited resource, on the one hand and widen the gap between the people and the administrator, on the other. Therefore, proper educational facilities to the rural masses may be given priority, which could create awareness and better response to lasting results, the authors suggested.

As regards the attitudes of Consolidation Department towards the scheme, the authors point out that almost all the respondents report in favour of an ordinance on consolidation with necessary amendments. Further, fifty percent of the respondents suggest magisterial intervention to compel the owners to continue in the scheme once they exercise their consent and the right of appeal should be withdrawn. Suggestions for amending the ordinance, however, throws significant light on the extreme importance of the attitudinal pre-requisites, which are necessary on the part of administrators and other, who are engaged in pursuing and in implementing such an ameliorative measure as a part of land reforms programme. Accordingly, ordinances must be drawn up which can at least restore faith of the people in such programme. The authors rightly suggest for generation of enthusiasm for effecting reforms and creation of proper attitudinal environment. Besides, the role of administrators is also extremely in the creation of a congenial climate conducive to bring an end to the hindrances in implementing the scheme, the authors emphasize.

5.2 Short-Term Effects of Consolidation of Holdings

Studies which focused on the short-term economic and social impact of land consolidation are detailed below.

Bansil (1959) [4] analyzed the structure of land holding pattern in India and the relevance of consolidation of land holdings to agriculture. The author rightly points out that India is a land of small holdings. The important factors responsible for such fragmentation of land holdings, are: the laws of succession/inheritance, population growth and absence of alternative occupation to absorb growing population. Accordingly, the author suggests a number of remedial measures to operationalize the Land Consolidation Scheme and also for preventing such fragmentation.

Firstly, it is suggested that the consolidation should be sustained by altering the inheritance laws of the Hindu Code which gives property rights to daughters along with sons. If change of inheritance laws is not possible, it is desirable to prevent it at least in the consolidated areas through suitable legislations.

Secondly, consolidation programme must gain in pace. Wide publicity about the gains accruing from consolidation further stimulates initiative and strengthens farming activities. The existence of service co-operatives in the areas where consolidation has taken place should also accentuate those gains.

Thirdly, it is suggested that the siphoning of the surplus population from agriculture to industries located either in rural or in urban areas would weaken their sentimental attachment to ancestral land properties and their desire to cling even to the tiniest holdings, irrespective of the economic value.

The analysis of Mann (1959) [5] on the impact of land consolidation reveals that consolidation of land holdings leads to: (i) increase in cultivable acreage due to reduction in unnecessary boundary ridges, wasteland and reduction in number of fragmented plots; (ii) decrease in time, energy and efforts to till the land; (iii) increase in intensive cultivation; (iv) increase in operational efficiency; and (v) enlarging the land for application of modern technology and reaping higher yield. In addition to the above benefits, it also enables farmers to erect high bunds around their compact blocks to protect their land from soil erosion and to harvest and preserve rain water. The study is a dynamic one from the point of view of environmental science, but the methodology adopted in the study is not sufficient to explore the socio-economic status of different size class farmers while enjoying the benefits of consolidation.

Planning Research and Action Institute (1961) [6] Lucknow, conducted an investigation on the impact of consolidation of holdings by drawing samples from two districts of Uttar Pradesh. The study reveals that consolidation has significant impact on the use of seed, organic manures and irrigation well. The use of these inputs has increased intensively in project area (consolidated area) compared to that in control area (unconsolidated area). The study is more pragmatic from the point of view of resource use.

Shetty (1963) [7] analyzed the working of the Consolidation Act, 1963 in three districts of Mysore State, namely, Bijapur, Belgaum and Dharwad. To know the impact of consolidation, the average size of scattered holdings and also the average number of scattered plots per holding, both before and after consolidation and the extent of consolidation were examined. The analysis reveals that a large majority of villages in Belgaum district show 50 to 75 percent reduction in the total number of fragments; but in Bijapur district only 27 percent in Indi Taluka and 31 percent in Bagewadi Taluka shows similar reduction. An interesting point which throws some light on the fact is that even after consolidation, a large number of fragments remain as they are.

The study is made to know why consolidation does not remove the fragments completely in spite of the fact that they are considered uneconomic from the point of view of cultivation. It revealed the peculiar advantages of non-consolidation and fragmented pieces of land benefit to the land owner in various ways.

First, the difference in the quality of soil in two fragmented plots enables the farmer to go for cultivation of different crops.

Second, scattered land holdings mean less risk of crop failure in the event of natural calamities, for which land owners concerned do not agree to exchange them.

Third, the analysis reveals that owners of the plots which are very close to their houses are naturally reluctant to exchange them for plots lying far off. However, this does not mean that consolidation is never advantageous. Both the consolidated and fragmented holdings are advantageous. Therefore, the author rightly emphasizes in this connection that a comprehensive programme of agricultural improvement must accompany consolidation programme if it is to prove really advantageous to the farmers. The issues relevant to land consolidation need to be well addressed in policy perspective in the context of its advantages and disadvantages, the author concludes.

The study of Padki (1965) [8] on a village in Maharashtra revealed a spectacular change in the size and number of plots due to consolidation. The analysis of his data shows that after consolidation the number of plots below the standard area of 2 acres appears to have reduced from 1,807 in number to 809. The average size of fragmented land area below the standard area appears to have increased from 0.47 acre to 0.74 acre. The average size of plots above the standard area had increased from 3.85 acres to 4.14 acres. The study emphasizes that consolidation tends to enlarge the holding size and paves the way for application of modern technology to reap higher output.

Sreeram's study (1966) [9] on 14 villages in Uttar Pradesh revealed that social gains and economic advantages of land consolidation appears to have increased significantly through transformation effects. Due to consolidation, the village lay-out and the shape of the country-side undergo spectacular change. The introduction of consolidation scheme in those villages restructure the village and country-side by reserving land for common and socially useful purposes, such as for community centres, hospitals, playground, burial ground etc. and make provision for spreading the network of roads, drainage and irrigation channels etc. Besides the above social gains and administrative advantages, consolidation leads to increase in economic gains in the form of extension of chaka roads, pathways and straight irrigation canals to the agricultural fields.

All these have resulted in the reduction of supervising time, transportation cost of carrying farm inputs and implements. However, the analysis of his field data reveals that supervising cost and time have been reduced from ₹ 100 and 60 man-days respectively in unconsolidated area to ₹ 20 and 10 man-days respectively in consolidated area. While the rice and wheat production per acre increased from 9.75 and 11.20 maunds in unconsolidated area to 11.25 and 12 maunds respectively in consolidated area, a noticeable change also occurred in crop intensity, the study revealed.

A review of performance of the Scheme of Consolidation of Land Holdings by the Land Reforms Implementation Committee of the National Development Council, Planning Commission, Government of India (1966) [10] emphasized on the need of keeping the land records updated and carrying out of the preparation of revision of land records as the pre-requisite conditions for the smooth and successful implementation of a land reform measure. In the absence of such updated land records of the land owners and tenants, it is very difficult to implement any such popular scheme and programme and also in establishing the right to title of holding and facilitating the exchange of land between the title holders or land owners in the process of consolidation. The Committee also emphasizes that other developmental plan and programmes like the plan of developing irrigation and drainage projects should go hand in hand with the programme of land consolidation to reap the higher benefits in agriculture. Because irrigation appears to be a major cause of promoting gains from consolidation of land, in the absence of irrigation water, consolidated land may fail to fetch higher yield, the Committee stressed.

A study made by Dutta (1968) [11] shows that there is popular thinking among the farming community that marginal and small farm holders do not get fair justice during exchange of plots during consolidation proceedings. The programme is heavily weighed in favour of big land owners as the corrupt officials show much favour and inclination to them while paying no heed to protect the interests of marginal and small farmers.

Mavalankar (1971) [12] reviewed the case study titled

'Economics of Land Consolidation in India' made by S.K. Agarwal and holds the view that the study is comprehensive and genuine one in analyzing the impact of land consolidation on a number of aspects encompassing land use pattern, cost per acre of land, yield per acre, use of inputs like seeds, fertilizer, improved farm machineries and implements, plant protection devices, labour utilization pattern etc. But, the review points out that the peculiar aspects of the agricultural subsistence economy have not been taken into account by the case study of Agarwal. That a scattered and fragmented land holding could make up for the loss of crop failure due to any reason at one place/parcel by obtaining a huge gain at some other parcel/place due to bumper crop etc.

Jacoby and Jacoby (1971) [13] attempted to evaluate the impact of land consolidation in excessively fragmented area of Sudan and U.A.R. The Gazire Scheme in Sudan, a large-scale consolidation scheme, was taken for the study to know the impact of this scheme on agriculture. The study shows that the conversion of large number of fragmented small units of land into a few number of big rectangular size of land on account of consolidation, saves time, energy and reduces endless walking hours of moving agricultural implements, human labour, bullocks and farm inputs from plot to another. Those large size plots also pave the way for spreading the network of irrigation —water canal easily flows across the fields without any loss of much water as happened earlier. Besides, it also leads to the economic use of water, farm inputs and pest control more effectively and maximization of output is achieved through the application of modern and new technology.

The National Commission on Agriculture (1976) [14] in submitting its report observed that consolidation tends to provide land of uniform size and in rectangular shape. It makes provision of straight access road/path and irrigation canal across the field which in turn saves supervising time and energy and leads to economic use of material input resources. Besides, it enhances the operational and management efficiency of the farm holders which results in earning higher yield and profit.

Singh, Jasbir (1976) [15] examined the effects of consolidation of holdings on agriculture in village Malikpur of Thaneswar Tehsil in Kurukshetra district and village Chatiaaulia under Tehsil and district Sonipat in Haryana state. As a result of consolidation, the number of plots has reduced, and instead of irregular fields, there is regular shape of the fields demarcated in rectangles with straight roads linking the villages with the fields. It is reported that installation of the number of tube wells has increased from a negligible number to 24 after consolidation. This is true in case of most of the villages in the North-east of Haryana where tube wells are the primary source of irrigation. In the canal irrigated areas, consolidated plots also appear to have enjoyed the benefit of canal irrigation. Other advantages of consolidation of holdings are manifold: improved operational efficiency besides cultivation being extended and intensified and land development plans are implemented. The plans implemented cause a host of social gains and administrative advantages. The increase in agricultural production (due to consolidation of land alone) without change in techniques has been 25 percent, Singh claims.

Singh, A. (1978) [16] observed that consolidation benefits the big or large farm holders more than the marginal and small farm holders. The officers and staff of the Consolidation Department show undue favour to the big and large farm holders at the cost of marginal and small farm holders though the latter constitute the largest section of the farming community. He suggests for taking care of the interest and concurrence of the marginal and small farmers for the smooth and successful implementation and operation of consolidation scheme.

Singh, Charan (1986) [17] reported the impact of consolidation of holdings in Uttar Pradesh and points out that consolidation of holding is understood to have a number of socio-economic advantages compared to the disadvantages of fragmentation of land holdings. The advantages of consolidation are, extension of cultivable land as a result of reduction of waste land and abolition of superfluous boundaries, efficient supervision and management of farm operation, efficient management of crop protection, reduction in land litigation and reduction in wastage of time and energy due to labour and bullock shifting from plot to plot. In Domariaganj, a Tehsil of Basti District, it is reported that when thirty plots are consolidated into two or three bigger compact plots, the quantum of human labour which goes in waste in the past has been saved. The impact of consolidation is quite apparent in 75 percent villages in Aligarh District in 1963-64 where, in one village 28 new wells are sunk on consolidated lands. At that time, 2 lakh of the 5 lakh irrigated acres of land get water from surface wells, thus leading to expansion of need-based irrigation within the control of the farmers.

Dash, Giridhari (1889) [18] evaluated the consolidation of holdings programme in Orissa implemented since January 1973 covering an area of about 5.70 lakh hectares in 4,264 villages in the District of Cuttack, Puri, Balasore, Ganjam, Keonjhar, Dhenkanal, Sambalpur, Bolangiri and Mayurbhanj. While critically evaluating the operation of the programme he observes that apart from aiming at boosting agricultural production, the programme envisages restructuring of the village landscape. He reports that consolidation programme has opened up new vistas like introduction of modern technology, encouragement to install private source of irrigation and availability of more cultivable land by reduction of number of ridges.

In the irrigated areas, introduction of field channels led to uniformity in distribution of water and minimization of wastage of water. With the reduction of boundary lines, litigation on account of field boundary disputes has been minimized. Apart from this, the programme is found to have generated substantial employment opportunities to the unskilled category of labour to undertake various farm activities consequent upon the development of irrigation and cropping intensity. Villagers' participation in the programme and mandatory provisions to consult them at various stages of consolidation has led to a revival of village Panchayat system, where the village body has a major say in the affairs of the village concerning implementation of the Scheme. Primarily, the programme aims at settlement of disputes through reconciliations and negotiations so as to minimize disputes.

Dash concluded that implementation of the programme has not been very satisfactory as anticipated. He suggests that the success of the programme depends upon the adoption of modern practices in agriculture, mechanization, installation of private source of irrigation etc.

In a State like Orissa, where a majority (83.4 percent of total cultivators) of farmers being small and marginal and where the modernization of agriculture has remained far from reality the advantages of consolidation have not been properly disseminated. However, despite the above constraints, the consolidation Scheme is gaining popularity and its acceptability has increased, Dash reveals.

Singh, Pritam (1989) [19] unveiled the history of consolidation of holdings and assesses the impact of consolidation of village Ghungrali of Ludhiana district in Punjab. He reports that consolidation of holdings has played a major role in ushering the *green revolution* in the Punjab. The adoption of new technology, which is also known as seed-cum-fertilizer-cum-pumping sets technology, which revolutionized the production potential, is made possible due to the investment climate created by the consolidation of holdings. Singh reports about some socio-economic advantages of consolidation in Punjab. With four exhaustive tables, he presented the data showing the year-wise progress of consolidation from 1950-51 to 1985-86 and the year-wise cultivable area added during the same period as a result of consolidation.

Singh also reports that in Samrala Tehsil of Ludhiana district, consolidation operation was completed in 1954 and

750 percolation wells were sunk and 230 tube wells and pumping sets were installed within a year. Besides socio-economic advantage the social gains like replanning of the country-side and provision of road communication has increased in Punjab after consolidation. It is due to the consolidation of holdings in Punjab that "as one flies from Calcutta to Amritsar, the rural landscape from Delhi onwards shows a marked change. One finds today, large areas demarcated in rectangles with straight roads linking the villages with the fields and market towns", Singh claims.

Chawla and Chahal (1989) [20] examined the effect of the 'Consolidation of Land Holding Act of 1948' on the size of the holding, number of plots per holding and the size of plots in Punjab. They also analysed the reasons and accounts for the reappearance of the process of deconsolidation in one of the districts, Amritsar of Punjab state. For the study, 108 cultivators from six villages under three development Blocks of Tehsil Tarn Taran of District Amritsar were selected randomly. To ascertain the impact of consolidation, the year 1961-62 (5 years after consolidation) has been compared with the 1951-52 (5 years before consolidation) in respect of holding size, number and size of plots in the holding and other parameters of agricultural production. In the post-consolidation period, number of plots per holder ranges between 0.26 and 3.0, while the size of the plot stands between 2.67 and 7.29 acres. Therefore, consolidation has no doubt affected the number and size of plots on all types of land operation, owned and leased.

The study further reveals that lately, there has been a tendency towards deconsolidation. Among the factors responsible for the process of deconsolidation, inheritance and sale and purchase transaction were found important.

Sharma (1990) [21] examined the post-consolidation situation in two typical villages viz. Jumuli Kalan and Bagahi under Balampur Pargana in Ganda district of Uttar Pradesh during 1979-80. He discovered a remarkable change with regard to land use and cropping patterns. Consolidation has also increased the size of the holding, facilitating better access to land for enabling to reap the fruits of large-scale production.

Mishra (1990) [22] critically evaluated the consolidation operation in Orissa initiated by the legislation in 1972 and he observed that consolidation seems to have been undertaken only for the sake of consolidation, but not for a radical agricultural transformation. However, from the point of view of agricultural growth with social justice, ceiling and land consolidation must go side by side. Mishra also observed that in Orissa the consolidation laws have helped the growth of corruption, nepotism and arbitrariness in the process of implementation and as such, have retarded the progress of implementation of Programme and seem to have diluted the true objectives of land consolidation.

Prasad (1992) [23] in his research study very meticulously analyzed the pre-consolidation (1972-73) and the post-consolidation (1987-88) land use situations in the Chandauli Tehsil of Varanasi District in Uttar Pradesh and makes an assessment of the impact of consolidation on a typical rural landscape of the middle Ganga Plain. A study of the pre- and post-consolidation land use shows that consolidation has resulted in a number of changes in land use pattern. These changes are: (i) changes in the number of land holdings and field plots; (ii) changes in size of plots; (iii) changes in field pattern, (iv) changes in agricultural land use; and (v) changes in non-agricultural land use pattern.

The analysis reveals that after consolidation the holdings have been brought together, thus, reducing their number. On an average, 2 to 3 holdings have been allotted to each owner after consolidation, taking into account factors like irrigation, double-cropping, lines of communication and distance from a settlement or abadi. In the sample villages as a whole, the average size of plot was 0.12 hectare before consolidation as compared to 0.22 hectare after consolidation. Consolidation has also caused a change in the shape of plot and field boundaries. Village studies have shown contradictory result with regard to net areas sown. In some villages, the net area sown has decreased after consolidation due to allotment of some agricultural land for non-agricultural uses like chaka roads, thrashing ground, water channels etc.

However, in some other villages like Kalyanpur Khurd and Musafapur, it has increased slightly due to reclamation of cultivable waste. As a result of consolidation, there has been a decrease in the area of fallow land by 3.22 percent from 4,350 hectares before consolidation (1972-73) to 4,210 hectares (1987-88) after consolidation. The author's analysis reveals that the area sown more than once under double and triple cropping has increased from 19.66 percent to 56.04 percent in all the villages under study after consolidation. But the area under single cropping has decreased in all sample villages ranging from 47.29 percent to 12.54 percent. The gross sown area has increased in all the villages ranging from 5 percent to 9.14 percent. Area under Kharif crops increased after consolidation in all the villages ranging from 3.12 percent to 31.64 percent. This is because of increase in area under paddy. Precisely therefore, consolidation of holding pattern of land holding has multiplied cultivated area and has enabled double/triple cropping due to better irrigation, the author argues.

The analysis further reveals that the area under HYV paddy with a higher yield as compared to early paddy has increased in all the villages because of rapid development of irrigational facilities in the post-consolidation period. The area under arhar, an annual crop, has generally gone down on account of its partial replacement by other crops following improved irrigation facilities. The area under sugarcane in villages under study, has increased on account of rise in demand and price level and improved irrigation facilities. Area under Rabi crop has registered a decrease in all the blocks except in Kalyanpur and Khurd and Chilbilli due to temporary shortfall in the available irrigation facilities but crops like wheat and potatoes have registered a remarkable increase in all the villages.

The area under non-agricultural land use as a whole has increased in almost all the villages mainly due to the provision for reserving land for common threshing ground, compost pit, playground, chaka road, chaka water channel etc. The village Naikot and Chilbilli recorded an increase in grove and pasture. However, there was a decline in waste land in village Naikot, Chilbilli and Mustafapur due to reclamation of land. The area under settlement has increased in all the villages.

Besides these, consolidation has also resulted in considerable changes in social gains like: (i) village layout, (ii) labour cost, (iii) irrigation facility, (iv) level of mechanization, (v) crop and agricultural productivity, (vi) caloric availability, (vii) per capita caloric intake, (vii) modernization of agriculture, and (ix) rise in the economic status of the villages etc. With the increase in the size of land holdings, greater utilization of irrigational facilities has become economically feasible. The study reveals an improvement in the level of mechanization in the form of an increase in the use of manures and fertilizers, an increase in ploughing intensity and an increase in the use of modern farm implements during post-consolidation period. With the increase in irrigation potential and level of mechanization, the crop yield and agricultural productivity has increased. As a result, the economic standard of living of the people of the consolidated villages has increased. The study also reveals that consolidation has brought spectacular changes in the village life and improvement in the level of living of the people.

Prasad, on the basis of his research work, succeeded in showing how the process of consolidation has led to an increase in land use efficiency in the area. He has put forward sound and timely suggestions for better land use planning with a view to promoting the quality of life of the people.

Ballabh and Walker (1992) [24] made an in-depth study of various aspects of both land fragmentation and land consolidation in dry semi-arid tropics (SAT) of India. Their analysis reveals that in most parts of India's dry SAT area, fragmentation is not posing any serious problem. In those areas, untapped resources are not abundant compared to other parts of the country. In Eastern part of India, consolidation of land could lead to harnessing of under utilized ground water resources. This is because consolidation provides farmers with ample opportunities to increase their private investment on tube well irrigation for proper water management. It also facilitates improvements in market access, reduction in the cost and time of labour supervision, increase in the operation efficiency of farm etc. The author suggests that consolidation may not be accorded high priority in India's dry semi-arid tropics.

Singh, Brijpal (1993) [25] analyzed the main factors responsible for astounding success of consolidation of holdings in Punjab and opines that the Punjab experience of consolidation of holdings should provide lessons for Bihar and other States. He observes that the success in Punjab is attributable to an interesting combination of factors including the interest and involvement of the people and the vision and the confidence of the administration. Such astounding success can be attributed to the commitment and vision of the political leaders of the State like Giani Kartar Singh and Pratap Singh Kairon and Others. Singh, however, brings out some of the important socio-economic advantages of consolidation accrued in the State of Punjab. Those are, namely, a general increase in cultivable acreage as a result of reduction of boundaries and waste lands, reduction in land leased out and resuming cultivation by owner-cultivators not cultivating earlier, and increase in private investment in irrigation which includes sinking of tube wells and better utilization of canal irrigation and increase in private investment in land development. The most important social gain is the re-planning of countryside, which includes planning of sites and reserving land for housing, social institutions such as educational institutions, hospitals, dispensaries, community centres, places of worship, playground, cremation ground and the provision of network of road communications, drainage and irrigation canals etc.

Das, Arunima (1993) [26] examined the impact of consolidation on agriculture and resource use in Pattamundai Tehsil of Cuttack District in Orissa. Two villages, one each from consolidation area and non-consolidated area were chosen randomly for the purpose of this case study. It is reported that in all types of holdings, yield of paddy and of pulse in consolidated village was more than that of non-consolidated village.

The author reports that the use of human labour per acre is 47.7 person days in consolidated villages and 50.8 in non-consolidated villages. Thus, the average utilization of labour per acre by cultivators in the consolidated are is less than that of non-consolidated area. Irrespective of holding sizes, about 2.9 labour days per acre are saved when the holdings are consolidated. Similarly, the number of bullock labour days used is 7.19 per acre in consolidated area in comparison to 8 days in non-consolidated area. Thus, use of labour resource is lower in consolidated area. It is also reported that the average cost of production of paddy and pulses per quintal in consolidated villages is lower than that of unconsolidated villages. The author rightly points out that there is a saving in bullock and human labour as a result of consolidation and the resource so released is certainly available for fruitful employment elsewhere and therefore, additional job opportunities for this purpose should be worked out in future planning.

However, the major causes attributed to the relative advantages of the former type over the latter have not been addressed in the study report. It is proposed to make an attempt in our empirical exercise to take care of the unexplored research questions of the author in the context of the relative advantages/disadvantages of the consolidated holdings over the non-consolidated ones.

Jena, Sadangi and Swain (1997) [27] examined the impact of land consolidation on farming community of Puri district in Orissa. Their study makes an attempt to assess the socio-economic advantages of land consolidation in Orissa.

The major findings emanating out of the study are: (i) consolidation has helped the marginal farmers in a big way to raise significantly the cropping intensity, area under HYV paddy, fertilizer consumption and recurring farm investment; (ii) the small farmers too are influenced greatly by the land consolidation. They could achieve significant higher annual farm income without much increase in recurring investment; (iii) among the socio-economic advantages, number of scattered plots reduced significantly, significant increase in cost of land and area under land development, difficulty in farm supervision reduces greatly and greater wastage of the small farmers reduces greatly.

However, the major advantages of consolidation in terms of higher cropping intensity, annual farm income, crop diversification and other socio-economic benefits are very rightly studied by the author, but whether consolidation of holdings as a type of institutional reform has really enabled/empowered the small land holders to use better scientific farm technology, modern farm and irrigation assets and HYV seeds, fertilizer, pesticides in their consolidated holdings to reap the benefits in a big way (compared to unconsolidated holdings) have remained unexplored and needs to be explored for strengthening the argument in favour of consolidation of holdings in Orissa.

ASCI, (2000) [28] conducted a study to review the progress of the performance of the Scheme "Consolidation of Land Holdings" and Computerization of Land Records in 10 (ten) States and to document the efforts made on consolidation and computerization in various States by the Ministry of Rural Development, Government of India. ASCI carried out the 'spot study' on the progress of Land Consolidation and Computerization of Land Records in ten States. The final report by the ASCI has since been received, who have recommended that there is no need of a Centrally Sponsored Scheme on Consolidation of Land Holdings.

However, the States of their own could initiate and carry out the programme of consolidation whole-heartedly for the development of agriculture, which is a State subject. The study report reveals that the Scheme of Consolidation of Land Holdings as a part of land reform measures has become very successful and popular in the States such as Punjab, Haryana and Uttar Pradesh. Having drawn the lessons of gain realized in those States, some States like Bihar, Gujarat, Madhya Pradesh and Maharashtra implemented this conception, but could not continue with it due to various administrative complications and public agitations. It is observed that the political ideology did not support this Scheme to be implemented in some States like West Bengal. There is legislation on the consolidation of land holdings in Tamil Nadu and this Scheme has not been conceived and implemented in the State.

In most of the tribal dominated North Eastern Hilly States of India, the application of the Scheme of Consolidation has become either irrelevant or not feasible due to enjoyment of communal ownership of land by the tribes, difference in quality of land due to difference in terrain and topographical location of land in those States. The Scheme of Consolidation of Land Holdings has been made voluntary in large number of States and this has evoked enough of people's participation to make it a success.

Mohanty (2001), [29] in his study on 'Land Reforms in Orissa', examined the impact of consolidation of holdings on the aspects of household income, labour productivity, employment generation, asset creation and technology adoption by drawing sample households from two districts, viz. Cuttack and Sonepur. His study reveals that consolidation helps raising household income, labour productivity, employment of family labour in farm, asset creation and technology adoption by sample households.

However, the increase in each of the variables due to consolidation is felt larger among the sample households in the least developed district, Sonepur than the most developed district, Cuttack. Mohanty concluded that the farm households of the less developed districts are more directly benefited from consolidation than their counterparts in the more developed districts. This is because land owning farm households of a least developed district like Sonepur accept agriculture as the main source of livelihood and take much care of cultivation whereas land owning farm households of most developed district like Cuttack receive regular income from certain non-farming activities in addition to agriculture. The households of Cuttack district assume agriculture as a subsidiary occupation and lay less emphasis on cultivation.

In spite of the revelation of significant impact of land consolidation, some deficiencies are discernible in Mohnty's study.

First, a methodological point—as we all know the impact of any change can be analysed by two methods, viz. 'before and after' and 'with-or-without'. Each method has, some disadvantages but the 'with-or-without' method (here villages with consolidation and villages without consolidation) is often preferred to 'before and after' (here pre-consolidation and post-consolidation period) method as the latter method cannot control variation in other conditions before and after and which is also entirely dependent on the memory of the respondents in the study area. But here, Mohanty has not taken into consideration the 'with or without' method, i.e. he has not made a comparative study between the sample households of consolidated villages and unconsolidated villages.

Second, by adopting 'size class index method' he has not made a comparative study between the intra-size class households as whether large farm households or small farm households are getting more benefits from the consolidation while making pre- and post-consolidation period analysis in consolidated villages.

Third, he has also not made a comparative study of households between irrigated and un-irrigated villages by taking into account irrigation, which is a major cause of promoting gains from consolidation.

Fourth, he has not adopted 'income group index method' simultaneously with 'size-class index method', which is more scientific and logical to explore the socio-economic status of households, and their investible surplus in order to ascertain whether higher income group households are at an advantage to appropriate benefits of the consolidation due to application of better farm technology/farm mechanization and effective use of irrigation water. These aspects are not well captured in the size class index as we notice very higher income group households in the lower size-class may be due to fertile land, better irrigation and intensification of family labour besides huge non-farm sources of income.

Padhy and Rani (2004) [30], while analyzing land reforms in Orissa, observe that consolidation of holdings is an ameliorative venture to the scattered nature of the agricultural holdings which possess a great impediment to land development and profitable agriculture. Consolidation aims at achieving compactness of agricultural holdings through a scheme of redistribution of land in compact rectangular blocks where feasible. In a broader sense, consolidation embraces an element of village planning, reservation of land for communal use and for future developmental purposes for better roads and communication facilities, irrigation and drainage channels. The entire scheme is to be implemented through the legal framework of the relevant act, with the active co-operation of a representative body of the villages. Due to consolidation, boundary lines are reduced in number and extent, releasing many additional acres for agriculture and bringing down boundary disputes.

Consolidation results in better management and supervision, increases profitability, stimulates land development and facilitates application of improved techniques of agriculture. They finally suggest that consolidation of land holdings as a part of land reform measures offers the maximum return to the tiller and raises their standard of living. In the context of agrarian economy of Orissa, the implementation of such a scheme assumes great significance. They observe that it is the peasant struggle in Orissa that has yielded the result of land reforms and the reforms in their turn have changed the social status of the people of Orissa. The analysis of Padhi and Rani is based upon the secondary data and it is lacking in empirical primary field data. The study is also deficient in evaluating the impact of the implementation of consolidation programme in Orissa.

So also in their reports, on consolidation of holdings in Kerala, Madhya Pradesh and Punjab, Jayachandran (1965), Jogelkar (1962) and Randhawa (1965) have assessed the organization progress, achievement and the impact of consolidation in those states respectively.

In contrast to all the above views, Sengupta (2004) [31] has put forth a dissenting view on land consolidation. He has presented available evidence which clearly suggests that the unqualified faith in the merit of consolidation is not justified. In such cases, fragmentation may have some rationale. Comparative benefits of fragmentation and consolidation need to be assessed carefully. He has presented the evidence given by McCloskey (1975, 1977) which states that there may be some rationale why peasants opt for scattering. Farmers protect themselves and their families from agricultural shocks by diversifying holdings among many small plots facing different weather, weed, water, rodent, insects and soil conditions. If one plot does poorly and another does well, a farmer can still harvest enough gain to survive from all of his plots put together. He has mentioned the application of general equilibrium models by Townsend (1993) to study land fragmentation as a portfolio diversification problem. He has also presented the conclusion of Nori et al. (1999) that land fragmentation is a conscious strategy by the people to diversify production, minimize risk and maximize total production. Sengupta's paper substantiates this position with a case study of a tank irrigated agricultural system in the Southern part of the Gangetic plain of Bihar State.

Thereafter, it locates fragmentation within the boarder context and analyses its role within a hierarchy of phenomena in the linked social and ecological local system. For this analysis, an evolutionary game model is used. It is revealed that fragmentation increases the resilience of community participation or the system of co-operation. The study concludes by suggesting an appropriate strategy for resilience management. The appropriate recommendation is that the development agencies should undertake such works that increase productivity. The agencies should let the farmers adapt to the situation and their participation flourish in its own way. If the farmers opt for fragmentation, they should be allowed to do that. Agencies should refrain from forcing consolidation here. If the farmers do not favour fragmentation, they should be allowed to consolidate. This is the nature of resilience management.

5.3 Long-term Effects of Consolidation of Holdings

There are very few studies, which focus on the long-term economic and social impact of consolidation—study by Agarwal (1966); Bonner (1987) and Mandal (2004) appears to be an exhaustive one. In point of fact, research studies on the long-term effect of consolidation on the agricultural system has virtually been neglected in India.

Agarwal (1966) [32] conducted an exhaustive research study on the long-term economic and social impact of land consolidation in Lucknow district in Uttar Pradesh in 1962. He compared five villages (Control Group of Villages), where consolidation proceeding is not undertaken with another five villages (Project Group of Villages) where consolidation was completed in 1954-55 at least five years earlier to the study. To know the after effects of consolidation, a group of 165 households from five villages of Project Group was selected by employing random sampling method. The advantages, which these households (from the Project Group) enjoy, are then compared to that of 153 households from Control Group of five other villages, where holdings are unconsolidated.

A comparison between the farmers belonging to the Project Group and those belonging to the Control Group is made with a view to ascertaining whether there is a perceptive gap in the productivity of land, use of modern technology in production including the use of improved seeds, chemical fertilizers and modern machineries and implements etc. (before and after consolidation of holdings in the consolidated villages). Similarly, a comparison is made between the present conditions in the consolidated villages on the one hand, and those in unconsolidated villages on the other.

Further, a comprehensive enquiry is made as regards the total and per acre value of inputs and outputs of different crops, use of irrigation, improved seeds, fertilizers, improved agricultural implements, plant protection devices; and in each comparison the condition of consolidation is found favourable. The assets and indebtedness of cultivators in the two groups are examined and it is found that the assets of the Project households had increased and their indebtedness had diminished, while the conditions of the Control Group were exactly the reverse.

The author points out that before consolidation, holdings are fragmented into as many as ten scattered holdings or more but after consolidation, the number of the fragmented holdings has been considerably reduced.

As regards the use of improved methods of technology in cultivation in Project and Control villages under study, the data reveals that the above modern methods are used to a very large extent by the cultivators of consolidated holdings than by those of the unconsolidated holdings. Precisely, the study suggests that consolidation achieves all the above advantages and still reduces expenses and increases the yield. The author reports that the consolidated villages derive a great deal of economic advantages, both in terms of income and farm employment.

More strikingly, consolidation leads to an improvement in operational efficiency, increase in cultivated area, better land use patterns, efficient farm management, improved supervision, and a great deal of social gains including development of village communications, planning of village abadi, and provision of social amenities and works of common utilities the study affirms.

In order to highlight the obstacles in the way of implementation of consolidation programme, the author seems to have made a lot of keen observations. These may be categorized as: (i) technical, (ii) administrative, and (iii) institutional. Under technical head, the problems like wrong selection of consolidation area, dilatory and un-phased procedure, incomplete and wrong maps and land records are found to be important.

Under administrative head, problems like inadequate and untimely supply of stationery, lack of sincerity on the part of consolidation staff and corrupt practices are ascertained. Under the institutional head, difficulties like lack of proper publicity, lack of public co-operation and factionalism and rivalry among the villagers in support and against the programme are categorically noticed.

In sum, the study rightly brings out the following major research findings: Consolidation results in: (i) an expansion of gross cultivable acreage; (ii) increase in gross irrigated area; (iii) reduction in number of plots; (iv) increase in size of plots; (v) decrease in input cost and increase in return of output; (vi) reduction in labour utilization; (vii) change in farm practices; (viii) increase in the use of fertilizer and insecticides; (ix) increase in the amount of assets; and (x) use of improved agricultural implements. Apart from these points, it is a comprehensive study on the economics of land consolidation. A critical review of the study made by Agarwal demonstrates a major deficiency that he has not focused any light on, regarding the advantages of the fragmented and scattered land holdings during the time of crop failure at one place (due to natural calamities or something else), while highlighting all the benefits and advantages of land consolidation. Second, the difference in the quality of soil in two fragmented plots enables the farmers to go for cultivation of different crops. This aspect of fragmented land has also been over looked by Agarwal.

Bonner (1987) [33] examines the long-term socio-economic impact of consolidation of holdings on the agricultural system in two Haryana villages namely Sikhpura and Jogipur in Kurukshetra district, demonstrating how these changes are in turn related to other changes in village economy and society. He examines the long-term impact of consolidation at two levels, at the family farm level and at the village life level. It is revealed that in addition to short-term benefits of consolidation, it also has far reaching long-term benefits having a significant economic and social impact on the agricultural system. They benefits are: (i) extension of cultivable acreage, (ii) expansion of irrigated area, (iii) specialization of cropping pattern, (iv) increase of cropping intensity, (v) increase in yield, (vi) shift from subsistence to market-oriented cash cropping, (vii) rise in the economic status of the villagers, (viii) a shift in economic basis of village from exchange in kind to cash transaction, and (ix) expansion of irrigation.

Expansion of irrigation, across the cultivated land in the village seems to have changed the nature of agricultural cropping system in four ways.

Firstly, as irrigation spreads, cropping pattern becomes more specialized. This has reduced a diversified cropping pattern and has correspondingly increased crop specialization.

Secondly, with increase in irrigation, cropping intensity increases.

Thirdly, the widespread use of irrigation leads to a shift from subsistence cropping to market-oriented cash cropping.

Fourthly, due to availability of irrigation water, agricultural system gets modernized as reflected by an increase in the use of chemical fertilizers, application of better plant protection methods, use of pesticides and insecticides and increase in the extent of use of modern farm implements and machineries.

The above four changes in the agricultural system has profound economic and social effects/implications on the village economy and society, though its implications are many and varied in the study report. Besides these, the other long-term effects of consolidation are, rise in the economic status of villagers and a shift from traditional caste based occupation to modern contract based wage-labour occupation. Besides this, mechanization of agriculture creates new job opportunities like tractor mechanics, instrument makers etc.

These jobs require mechanical and technical skills to maintain and repair other machines such as, tube well, diesel and electric motor pump-sets etc. All these jobs require technical training and technical education for operation.

Mandal (2004) [34], in his study, attempted to make a comprehensive analysis of some major aspects of land consolidation implemented in Orissa on the basis of available secondary and some primary data.

He conducted a micro level field study to evaluate the impact of land consolidation scheme on the firm economy; to examine the issue of distribution of the benefit of consolidated crop enterprise among the different size class of farmers and to study the impact of land consolidation on man-days of employment in farm operations by drawing samples from seven irrigated consolidated villages and three irrigated unconsolidated villages at random in Nimapara Block of Puri district of Orissa.

His study revealed that farm business income is higher in consolidated areas. There is an increase in employment of family labour along with enhanced per hectare net return.

However, Mandal's study is also not free from certain methodological defects.

Firstly, he has not adopted 'with-or-without' method for taking irrigation into consideration, which plays a crucial role in promoting gains from consolidation. Besides, he has not made a comparative study between irrigated consolidated land and un-irrigated consolidated land etc.

Secondly, he has also not taken into consideration the aspect of adoption of new technology as a possible factor for increasing the farm business income in his analysis.

Thirdly, he has also not adopted income group index method to explore the socio-economic conditions of the sample households along with size class index method as the former is less erroneous and more logical and scientific than the latter.

Fourthly, the study does not go deeper to make an intra-size class analysis as to whether it is the smaller size farm holder or larger size farm holder which indeed fetches higher per hectare farm business income.

A cursory review of above literature and articles suggests that much work has been done to know only the short-term impact of land consolidation on agriculture. Except in rare studies like the study of Bonner and of Agarwal, no exhaustive study is conducted to assess the long-term impact of land consolidation.

The current study proposes to make an attempt to examine the long-term impact of consolidation, particularly, the impact of land consolidation on adoption of new technology and agrarian change. It is, therefore, proposed to study the unexplored research questions with respect to various aspects of land consolidation.

The cursory review of relevant literature on various aspects of consolidation of holdings and its application in various States also suggests its grand success in some States like Punjab, Haryana and some part of Uttar Pradesh though many States have been somewhat hesitant to introduce consolidation of holding as a progressive reform measure in land to raise productivity and farm production through use of better irrigation and farm technology. Some authors also claim that such an institutional measure is cost effective and benefits the small holders most, in terms of higher yield and crop diversification. But, such a progressive reform in land has not been uniformly applied in all States since agriculture is a State subject.

End Notes

1. Kaushik, R.N. (1953), "Consolidation of Holdings in India", *Agricultural Situation in India,* Vol. VIII, No. 4, July, pp. 253-254.
2. Elder, J.W. (1962), "Land Consolidation in an Indian Village: A Case Study of the Consolidation of Holdings Act in Uttar Pradesh", *Economic Development and Cultural Change,* 11(1).
3. Rizvi, S.M.Z.; Sabzwari, M.A.; Sharif, C.M. (1965), "Consolidation of Holdings: A Study of the Process of Consolidation of Agricultural Holdings in Selected Villages of Peshwar District".
4. Bansil, P.C. (1959), "Consolidation of Holdings in India", *Agricultural Situation in India,* Vol. XIV, November, No. 8, pp. 855-885.
5. Mann, W.S. (1959), "Scope for Consolidation of Holdings and Soil Conservation and Its Impact on Agricultural Production", *The Indian Journal of Agricultural Economics*, Vol. XIV, No. 3, July-September, p. 66 and p. 69.
6. Planning, Research and Action Institute, Lucknow, (1961), 'Impact of Consolidation of Holdings'.
7. Shetty, V.V. (1963), "Consolidation of Holdings in Mysore State", *Indian Journal of Agricultural Economics,* Vol. XVII, April-June, No. 2, pp. 46-54.
8. Padki, M.B. (1965), "Consolidation of Holdings", *Agricultural Situation in India*, Vol. XX, No.5, pp. 305-308.
9. Sreeram, N. (1966), "A Note on Consolidation of Holdings in Uttar Pradesh: A Field Survey", *The Indian Journal of Economics*, Vol. XLVI, No. 183, April, pp. 485-487.
10. Planning Commission (1966), "Implementation of Land Reforms: A Review, Land Reforms Implementation Committee of the National Development Council, Government of India, New Delhi, August, p. 283.
11. Dutta, N.C. (1968), "Consolidation of Holdings" Land Problems and Land Reforms in Assam, S. Chand and Co. Ltd., New Delhi, pp. 112-113.
12. Mavlankar, N.A. (1971), "Economics of Land Consolidation in

India: A Case Study Reviewed", *Artha Vijnana*, Vol. XIII, No. 4, pp. 452-456.

13. Jacoby, E.H. and Jacoby C.F. (1971), "Land Consolidation: The Small Land Reform", Man and Land: The Fundamental Issue in Development, Andre Deutsch Ltd., London, pp. 269-270.
14. National Commission on Agriculture (1976), "Report of the National Commission on Agriculture," Part XV, *Agrarian Reforms*, p. 308 and pp. 323-328.
15. Singh, Jasbir (1976), "Consolidation of Holdings, Land Tenure and Size of Operational Holdings", An Agricultural Geography of Haryana, Bishal Publication, Kurukshetra.
16. Singh, A. (1978), "Land Consolidation Programme in Bihar", *Yojana*, Vol. XXII, No. 10, June 1-15, pp. 29-30.
17. Singh, Charan (1986), "Consolidation of Holdings" Land Reform in U.P. and the Kulaks, Vikas Publishing House Pvt. Ltd., New Delhi.
18. Dash, Giridhari (1989), "Consolidation of Holdings", The Land System and Land Reform in Orissa.
19. Singh, Pritam (1989), "Consolidation of Holdings in Punjab", *Yojana*, Vol. 33, No.11, June 16-30, pp. 18-21.
20. Chawla, J.S. and Chahal T.S. (1989), "Consolidation of Holdings in Punjab and its aftermath", Land Reforms in India: Achievement, Problems and Prospects (eds.) M.L. Sharma and R.K. Punia, Ajanta Publication, India, pp. 113-124.
21. Sharma, S.C. (1990), "Post-Consolidation changes in the use of Land in Balarampur Pargana (Uttar Pradesh)", *Land Utilization and Management in India*, (ed.) Mishra, B.N., Chugh Publications, Allahabad.
22. Mishra, Krushna Chandra (1990), "Consolidation of Holdings", Land System and Land Reforms, Himalaya Publishing House, Delhi, pp. 542-544.
23. Prasad, Rama (1992), "Impact of Consolidation of Land Use", Printewell, Jaipur.
24. Ballabh, V. and Walker, T.S. (1992), "Land Fragmentation and Consolidation in Dry Semi-Arid Tropics of India", *Artha Vijana*, Vol. 34, No. 4, December, pp. 271-373.
25. Singh, Brijpal (1993), "Consolidation of Land Holdings in Punjab: Lessons for Bihar", Land Reforms in India: Bihar, Institutional Constraints, Sage Publications, New Delhi.
26. Das Arunima (1994), "Impact of Consolidation on Agriculture

and Resource Use: A Case Study in Pattamundai Tehsil", Department of Economics, Utkal University.
27. Jena, R.K., Sadangi B.N. and Swain P. (1997), "Impact of Land Consolidation in Farming", *Agricultural Situation in India*, May, Government of India, pp. 81-86.
28. Academic Staff College of India, Hyderabad (2000).
29. Mohanty, B.K. (2001), "Consolidation of Land Holdings in Orissa", Part IV, Land Reforms in Orissa, Unpublished ICCSSR Project, Cuttack.
30. Padhy, Subhash C. and Rani, A. Sobha (2004), "Peasants and Land Reforms in Orissa: 1936-1976", published by R.N. Bhattacharya, Kolkata.
31. Sengupta, Nirmal (2004), "Fragmented Landholding, Productivity and Resilience Management", *Environment and Development of Economics*, Vol. II, Part 4, August.
32. Agarwal, S.K. (1971), "Economics of Land Consolidation in India", S. Chand and Company Ltd., New Delhi.
33. Bonner, Jeffrey P. (1987), "Land Consolidation and Economic Development in India: A Study of Two Haryana Villages", Allied Publishers Pvt. Ltd., New Delhi.
34. Mandal, B. (2004), "Land Consolidation and Agricultural Development in Orissa: A Case Study Based on Puri District", Thesis submitted for the degree of Doctor of Philosophy in Economics to the Utkal University, Orissa.

6

Consolidation of Land Holdings: The Indian Experience

6.1 Reasons for Sub-division and Fragmentation of Holdings

The phenomenon of fragmentation of land holdings is widespread in India. The main reasons for sub-division and fragmentation of a single holding into a number of small and scattered strips of land often separated by long distances are possibly due to the following reasons:

1. Breaking up of joint family system and sub-division of land among family members owing to population explosion.
2. Extinction of families without direct heirs and the division of their properties amongst a large number of distant relatives.
3. Unrestricted transfer of land, frequent purchase and sale of land.
4. Rural indebtedness of poor farmers and sale of land to village money lenders
5. Inadequate opportunities in the field of non-agricultural employment.
6. Some of the land reform measures like abolition of intermediary in land, tenancy reforms, implementation of ceiling laws and redistribution of ceiling surplus land among landless have also indirectly contributed to the increase in the fragmented land holdings by creating a large number of ownership holdings.
7. The existence of absentee landlords and malafied transfers of the land by the big farmers to evade the ceiling on land holdings has also aggravated the fragmentation of land holdings.

The document of the Royal Commission on Agriculture

(1928) defined, "the fragmentation is accentuated by the expansion of cultivation, irregularity over the waste, by frequent purchase and sales of land and by extinction of families without direct heirs and the division of their properties amongst a large number of distant relatives. As a result, the agriculture holdings did not consist of a single compact block but also formed irregular shape" (FAO, 1955).

Consolidation of land holdings is designed to reverse the division and fragmentation of land into small units. Therefore, legislation on consolidation of land holdings is one of the important measures of land reforms in India. The legislative measures on consolidation consist of two parts: first, relates to prevention of fragmentation and the second deals with the procedure for the consolidation of holdings. Experience from the past has shown that state plays a significant role in the designing of the scheme of consolidation of land holdings and its implementation.

6.2 History of Consolidation of Land Holdings

Consolidation constitutes an important part of the land reform programmes initiated in many States in India. It is the most direct method of curing the evils of fragmentation. The expression 'consolidation of holding' refers to amalgamation and redistribution of land with a view to bringing together all plots of land of a cultivator in one compact block. Consolidation means "the re-arrangement of holdings in any area between several tenure holders in such a way as to make the holdings held by them more compact. The measure, thus, aims at giving every right holder a compact area equivalent in value to what he held before in scattered plots" (Government of India, Planning Commission, 1957, p. 2).

The main purpose of consolidation is to consolidate cultivation so as to save time and labour and at the same time to get a larger return for efforts and soil capital applied. Consolidation is a process of converting the pigmy holdings into economic ones by positive government action. Through the process of consolidation the scattered lands can be brought together. It is pre-requisite for modernized, mechanized and planned development of agriculture. It is primarily a production-oriented programme intended to play a significant role in re-shaping and remodelling the agrarian structure with a view to attaining a high degree of efficiency in economy. It has the great merit of increasing agricultural production on the one hand and reducing the cost on the other.

The origin of land consolidation dates back to mid-eighteenth century in Western Europe. "The concept of land consolidation has not only been interpreted to be only the simple reallocation of parcels to remove effects of fragmentation, it has also been associated with broader social and economic reforms from the time of its earliest applications in Western Europe. The first consolidation initiatives of Denmark in the 1750s were part of a profound social reform to free people from obligation to noble landlords by establishing privately-owned family farms. The consolidation of fragmented holdings did result in improved agricultural productivity". [1]

As reported, "Efforts at consolidating fragmented holdings of farmers were made in India before Independence and the two villages of the Central Provinces, one in Raipur district and the other in Bilaspur district were brought under the Scheme of Consolidation in 1905; of course on an experimental basis. Thereafter, in 1912, the then Director of Land Records and Agriculture in the United Provinces called attention of all concerned to the necessity for an extensive consolidation programme followed by the All India Board of Agriculture Report, 1917 and the Royal Commission on Agriculture Report, 1928 to adopt the said programme in order to prevent fragmentation of land holdings.

In the meantime, the Madras Government in 1911 initiated steps towards consolidation of land holdings. In response to the call given by the Director of Land Records and Agriculture and such other authorities, some provincial governments particularly of the Punjab, Uttar Pradesh made notable attempts to initiate measures of consolidation of scattered holdings. But, such measures were devoid of the element of compulsion. For example, the Uttar Pradesh Consolidation of Holdings Act No. VIII, 1939 proved ineffective because of its specifications that the measures of consolidation could be implemented in a village if one-third of the proprietors of the cultivated area of the village applied to consolidate their land holdings". [2]

In the Punjab, Hubert Calvert (I.C.S.), who served in the State from 1898 to 1933, was the pioneer of the consolidation of land holdings in the State. In 1921, he hit upon the discovery that co-operation could solve the problem of bringing together fragmented and scattered holdings of the farmers.

Under his instruction, the first co-operative society was formed in 1921, and in 1931 there were about 800 societies with 48,000 members. Describing the benefits of the consolidation of holdings, Sir Malcolm Darling stated, "in Gurdaspur, nearly 2,000 trees, including over 400 fruit trees, have been planted and forty nine manure pits have been dug.

However, the two commonest effects of consolidation are the sinking of wells and the bringing of waste land under cultivation.' From the experiences gained over the years, it was later decided that there should be some element of compulsion. Accordingly, the Punjab Consolidation Act, 1936 was passed, whereby consolidation work in a village could be undertaken, if two-thirds of the land owners give their consent. Soon after Independence, the necessity of the consolidation holdings was strongly realized and the East Punjab Holdings (Consolidation and Prevention of Fragmentation) Act was enacted in 1948 on the initiative of Gyani Kartar Singh, Revenue Minister of the State. An element of compulsion was introduced and, hence, the progress was rapid". [3] Having felt the necessity of bringing the households under the compulsion of consolidation of land holdings, several State governments in the post-Independence period enacted laws to prevent fragmentation of land holdings.

Among such Act, the foremost ones were the Bombay Prevention of Fragmentation and Consolidation of Holding Act, 1947 and the Utter Pradesh Consolidation of Holdings Act, 1953, the latter being contingent upon the Uttar Pradesh Zamindari Abolition and Land Reforms Act, 1951. All this is the evident of the role of States in the formation and implementation of the laws relating to prevention of fragmentation and consolidation of land holdings.

Consolidation has two types of objectives: (i) regrouping of scattered plots to form a compact block, and (ii) an integrated programme for rural development and reconstruction works of engineering and social importance. Consolidation Act has two parts: (a) one relates to prevention of fragmentation, and (b) the second deals with the procedure for consolidation of holdings.

6.3 Advantages of Consolidation of Land Holdings

6.3.1 Increase in Cultivable Acreage: Implementation of the scheme of consolidation has the advantage of reducing the number of fragmented plots and increasing the cultivable acreage. Due to consolidation, cultivable land area (sown area) increases as a result of reduction of wasteland, common grazing land, barren land, and abolition of superfluous boundaries. This naturally results in the enlargement of plots and reduction in the number of fragmented area which are below the standard area. The area of arable land increases, because abandoned tiny bits of land left out of cultivation (uncultivated land) are brought under plough after consolidation and fallow land are reclaimed. Reduction in the incidence of tenancy takes place as owner-cultivator stops leasing out distant plots and start cultivating his land when all his lands are brought at one place after consolidation. This brings a positive effect on the adoption of improved agricultural practices (increase in yield).

6.3.2 Increase in Operational Efficiency: Consolidation increases operational efficiency and managerial skill of the agricultural unit as fragmented plots are brought together into one compact block, even if the total size of the holding may not be increased. Cultivator exercises efficient supervision and management of farm operations. Consolidation makes the paths across village lands straight and short, which results in the reduction in wastage of time, energy in shifting of labour and bullocks from plot to plot. There is a great savings of time in seasonal crop inspections, which enables the senior revenue officers to exercise more effective supervision over their subordinates. A distinct shift from traditional agriculture to commercial agriculture is glaringly visible.

6.3.3 Reduction in Cost of Production: Consolidation reduces the cost of production. Due to consolidation, the cost of input for agriculture decreases. Labour utilization and capital duplication also reduces. Consolidation also influences the marginal farmers by: (a) raising significantly the cropping intensity, (b) raising area under H.Y.V. and, (c) raising fertilizer consumption per acre. Consolidation helps farmers to minimize recurring expenditures such as supervision, watching, weed control water management, labour management and drought power. Consolidation increases farm income of small and marginal farms.

6.3.4 Introduction of New Technology: Consolidation plays a significant role in introducing new technology, since a compact holding enables a cultivator to adopt improved methods of cultivation and better techniques. Consolidation creates investment climate for adoption of new technology which revolutionizes production potential of the farm. Consolidation gives rise to scientific ways of cultivation and improved methods. Due to consolidation, pathways or Chaka roads are laid easily and drainage irrigation channels are dug across the operated land due to its large size. This enables the farmers/cultivators to apply modern technology and use modern farm machinery and implements easily on farm land. It paves the way for modernization of farm technology and increases tractor cultivation. Per acre yield/output or return increases due to consolidation only, even if, without any change in technique of production. Consolidation leads to changes in land utilization, farm practices, cropping pattern (specialization of cropping patterns). Cropping intensity (growing of crops more than 2-3 times) increases. Seed and fertilizer costs, labour charges, and other forms of expenses are minimized. With straight water channels and evenly shaped fields, there is minor waste of irrigation water and increased convenience in use of water.

Cropping pattern changes from traditional food crops to cash crops which implies a shift from diversified crop (maize, gram etc.) production system to specialized crop (fine food grains like rice, wheat, sugarcane, cotton etc.) production system. The incidents of encroachment are reduced, which indirectly reduces boundary disputes and expensive litigation and reduces the number of visits to courts, revenue and tehsil offices. Cultivation is extended and intensified.

6.3.5 Expansion of Irrigation: Consolidation creates condition for rapid expansion of irrigation (both canal and lift irrigation) and irrigated areas and it makes a significant impact on minor irrigation facilities. It enables farmers to sink well and tube wells on their holdings. Consolidated plots enjoy the benefit to tube wells as well as canal irrigation. Irrigation spreads across a village and levels of micro-environmental variation is achieved. For irrigation purposes, Command Area Development Project and Land Development Plans are implemented by the government. CADA-Command Area Development Agency lays a network of channels throughout the consolidated area (Chakas) for better water management with less cost.

6.3.6 Social Gains: Consolidation leads to an increase in social gains and improvement in village layouts. Consolidation re-plans villages and the countryside by affording opportunities for developing the land, socially useful. Provision of social amenities improves. Re-planning of countryside includes planning of sites (reserving land) for housing, educational institutions, hospitals, dispensaries, community centres, places of worship, playground, burial ground and provision of network of roads, drainage and irrigation channels etc. Due to consolidation, social gains and administrative advantages are many and varied.

6.3.7 Occupational Changes: Along with social change, a spectacular change is noticed in the village life and it demonstrates a rapid expansion. Consolidation leads to changes in the nature of jajamani relations (occupational changes) or a shift in social relation—a shift from traditional caste occupation to contract case-wage (labour) occupation. It raises cost (valuation) of land and the psychological attachment to land. In a big farming community of India, the farmers possess different types of attitudes towards land consolidation due to the existence of different types of socio-economic and psychological background.

These human behavioural factors are instrumental components for either acceptance or rejection of the land consolidation programme. It provides psychological relief, mental satisfaction, economic security and a tension free life. It increases agricultural productivity, caloric availability and per capita calorie intake.

In brief, consolidation of land holdings has a great merit of increasing agricultural production in the following ways: first, consolidation leads to extension of cultivable area; second, it enhances the operational efficiency of the agricultural holdings; third, it paves the way for improvement and adoption of new technology; and fourth, it has social gains through transformation effects by replanning village and the countryside. These are elaborately discussed below.

Consolidation is instrumental in bringing socio-economic and technological changes among the farming community in different parts of the country. Due to consolidation some landless families secure some land from village common-land. It provides scope to some unskilled villagers to acquire training and skills to take up repairing and servicing activities of the farm machines and implements used by the cultivators.

Therefore, consolidation creates new job opportunities like tractor mechanics; repair mechanics, tube-well mechanics etc.

Indirectly, it raises literacy in imparting education and training, both general and vocational for improving the skills of those mechanics.

6.4 Legislative Provisions for Consolidation of Holdings in Different States of India

In India, 15 states and two union territories viz. Andhra Pradesh (Telangana Area), Assam, Bihar, Gujarat, Haryana, Himachal Pradesh, Jammu and Kashmir, Karnataka, Madhya Pradesh, Maharashtra, Odisha, Punjab, Rajasthan, Uttar Pradesh, West Bengal, Delhi (Union Territory) and Dadra & Nagar Haveli (Union Territory) have enacted legislations for carrying out consolidation of land holdings programme for prevention of further fragmentation of land. A list of the acts and legislative provisions enacted for consolidation operation by different State Governments and Union Territories is given in Table 6.1.

Among such Acts, the foremost ones are Bombay Prevention of Fragmentation and Consolidation of Holdings Act, 1947 for the States of Maharashtra and Gujarat; East Punjab Holdings (Consolidation and Prevention of Fragmentation) Act, 1948 for the States of Punjab and Haryana and Uttar Pradesh Consolidation of Holdings Act, 1953 for Uttar Pradesh, the latter being contingent upon the Uttar Pradesh Zamindari Abolition and Land Reforms Act, 1951.

Initially, most of the above states introduced the scheme of consolidation on voluntary basis, but later on, they made it mandatory. It has also been experienced by many states that compulsory consolidation of land holdings could make tremendous impact on the agrarian economy, especially when farmers are indifferent towards the voluntary consolidation.

The states, which have pursued this programme on compulsory basis have made substantial progress in the implementation of the scheme. All this suggests that the state has to play a crucial role in the formulation and implementation of the laws relating to prevention of fragmentation and consolidation of land holdings.

Table 6.1: Legislative Provisions for Consolidation of Holdings in Different States Till 1994

S. No.	State/Union Territory	Name of the Act
1.	Andhra Pradesh (*) (Telengana area only)	The Hyderabad Prevention of Fragmentation and Consolidation of Holdings Act, 1956
2.	Assam @	The Assam Consolidation of Holding Act, 1959 (Assam Act XIX of 1961)
3.	Bihar	The Bihar Consolidation of Holding and Prevention of Fragmentation Act, 1956
4.	Gujarat	The Bombay Prevention of Fragmentation and Consolidation of Holdings Act, 1947
5.	Haryana	The East Punjab Holdings (Consolidation and Prevention of Fragmentation) Act, 1948
6.	Himachal Pradesh	The Himachal Pradesh Consolidation of Holdings Act, 1953
7.	Jammu & Kashmir (*)	The Jammu and Kashmir Consolidation of Holding Act,1962
8.	Karnataka	(i) The Mysore Fragmentation and Consolidation of Holdings Bill, 1960;
		(ii) The Bombay Prevention of Fragmentation and Consolidation of Holdings Act, 1947
9.	Madhya Pradesh	The Madhya Pradesh Land Revenue Code, 1956, Chapter XVI
10.	Maharashtra	The Bombay Prevention of Fragmentation and Consolidation of Holdings Act, 1947
11.	Odisha	The Orissa Consolidation of Holdings and Prevention of Fragmentation of Land Act, 1972
12.	Punjab	The East Punjab Holdings (Consolidation and Prevention of Fragmentation) Act, 1948

Contd...

13.	Rajasthan	The Rajasthan Holdings (Consolidation and Prevention of Fragmentation) Act, 1948
14.	Uttar Pradesh	(i)The Uttar Pradesh Consolidation of Holdings Act,1953,
		(ii) The Uttar Pradesh Consolidation of Holdings Amendment Act, 1962
15.	West Bengal @	The West Bengal Land Reforms Act, 1955 (Relevant Sections only)
16.	Delhi	The East Punjab Holdings (Consolidation and Prevention of Fragmentation) Act, 1948 as extended to Delhi

(*) The Act has been kept in abeyance.
@ The Act has not been taken up for implementation.
Sources: Secondary published data from Ministry of Rural Development, Government of India, New Delhi; Final Report of Study on Review of Performance of Schemes of Consolidation of Land Holdings and Computerization of Land Records, Administrative Staff College of India, Hyderabad, December 2000.

On the basis of the information collected from the reports of the National Commission on Agriculture (NCA), (Government of India, 1976) and the report of the Administrative Staff College of India (ASCI) (Government of India, Ministry of Rural Development 2000), Indian states may be classified into six categories based on the enactment and implementation of the laws on consolidation of holdings. This classification is given as follows:

1. States in which commendable success and substantial progress has been made and which have plans for total coverage—Uttar Pradesh, Punjab and Haryana.
2. States in which substantial progress has been made in the implementation of this scheme in the early years of its inception, but the scheme has been subsequently discontinued due to various administrative complications, socio-economic problems and public agitations—Bihar, Gujarat, Maharashtra, Madhya Pradesh, Rajasthan and Karnataka.
3. States in which the scheme has been taken up on a large

scale and some progress is shown but total coverage is not yet completed—Himachal Pradesh and Odisha.

4. States in which experimental work has been done—Assam and Jammu & Kashmir.
5. States in which no progress has been made though legislative provisions exist—West Bengal and Andhra Pradesh.
6. States in which legislation has not so far been enacted—Tamil Nadu, Kerala, Sikkim and almost all the North-Eastern States like Arunachal Pradesh, Manipur, Meghalaya, Nagaland, Tripura and Mizoram. The conditions, the terrain, topography and the community nature of ownership of land in these States did not offer sufficient scope for introduction and the implementation of the Scheme of Consolidation. Consolidation of land holdings has also no relevance in those States.

6.5 Progress of Consolidation of Land Holdings

A cursory review of the performance and progress of implementation of consolidation scheme in different states shows that the work of consolidation of holdings has almost been completed in Uttar Pradesh, Punjab and Haryana and the scheme is still being carried out in some pockets of these States. In Odisha and Himachal Pradesh, consolidation work has been taken up on a large scale and the progress of consolidation has made some considerable progress in these States. In Gujarat, Madhya Pradesh, Maharashtra, Karnataka, Bihar and Rajasthan, appreciable work has been done and a substantial progress was observed in the early years of the implementation of the scheme. But the scheme has been discontinued in these states after experiencing various administrative complications and operational problems at the village and administrative level. The political ideology did not support this scheme to be implemented in some states like West Bengal.

Big states like Tamil Nadu, the Andhra area of Andhra

Pradesh, Kerala, Manipur, Tripura, Sikkim and Goa do not have legislative provisions for undertaking consolidation programme. Introduction of land consolidation in states of Kerala and Tamil Nadu was not possible due to large plantations of coconut and arecanut. In most of the tribal dominated North-Eastern States of India, the application of the scheme of consolidation has become either irrelevant or non-feasible due to enjoyment of communal ownership of land by the tribes, difference in quality of land, heterogeneity in terrain and topographical locations.

The study report of the Administrative Staff College of India (ASCI, 2000) recommended, "The approach to consolidation of land holdings depends largely on the uniformity of soil conditions, farm infrastructure, spatial features, cropping pattern and perceptions on the market value of the land and other associated factors. The scheme on consolidation of land holdings should be formulated with reference to the above factors specific to each state in a participatory manner. However, there is a need for formulating a National Policy on the consolidation of land holdings to provide a conceptual framework to the state governments on the subject. The policy needs to be judged by the states in the light of the various agronomic, market orientation, productivity based and social and cultural factors specific to the region". [4]

6.6 Reasons for Poor Performance

In India, consolidation of fragmented agricultural land holdings has been made an integral part of the land reform measures in the early post-Independence Planning period. The policy on consolidation of land holdings was conceptualized in the Second Five Year Plan. Since then, successive Five Year Plans have accordingly been laying stress on the implementation of the scheme consolidation of fragmented land holdings for planned development of villages and increased agricultural output. Since land reforms come under the purview of State List, many states had enacted legislations and had taken up the work relating to consolidation of land holdings. Punjab, Haryana, and Uttar Pradesh have achieved commendable success. In other States, consolidation drive continued for some years but lost momentum thereafter due to least concern for the implementation of the scheme owing to lack of political will and absence of rural leadership.

Besides, there are a few factors accounting for poor performance and these are discussed below:

1. Many State Governments seem to have been reluctant to implement, for fear of eviction of tenants and small and marginal farmers. It is feared that unless the tenant-at-will are registered and recorded, land consolidation may enable the big land owners to consolidate and convert their land holdings into large capitalist farms under the garb of personal cultivation and if necessary, by evicting tenants. The Task Force on Agrarian Relations (1973) observed that a major weakness of the programme was that consolidation was done without taking effective steps to ensure security to tenants. Thus, the fear of large scale ejectment of tenants seems to have slowed down the programme.
2. The need for minimum size of land holding according to the consolidation law also has posed some problems since bulk of land holdings in all states are of small size. Thus, need for legal provision arises to include small holdings or to go for some kind of co-operative arrangement by motivating small holders.
3. Lack of legal provisions for compulsory consolidation by the States.
4. Problem of proper valuation of each scattered plot of land to be consolidated and to be exchanged accordingly and lack of any reasonable criteria like land productivity, soil type, up land-low land situations etc. seem to have restricted/prevented farmers for exchange.
5. Lack of updated land records, trained staff and financial

problems of the State governments also showered down the progress of consolidation process. However, the Government of India still envisages the need for implementation of this scheme.

A report of the Administrative Staff College of India (ASCI, 2000), Government of India noted, "Consolidation of agricultural holdings, though not a measure to redistribute land but is considered necessary for planning development of villages and achieving higher level efficiency and economy in farm sector. This measure assumes added importance in the Indian context since the average size of operational holdings in the country is very low and under-sized holdings in the country are very large in numbers and these under-sized holdings are highly fragmented. This programme, therefore, forms an integral part of land reforms and successive Five Year Plans accordingly have been laying stress on the importance of its implementation. In pursuance of this strategy, a number of states have enacted legislation for carrying out consolidation of holdings but all of them have not pursued its implementation with equal vigour". [5]

There are many procedural problems in implementation of the Scheme in different states of the Country. The scheme has been implemented in some states on compulsory basis and in large number of states it has been voluntary. However, the scheme has been well implemented in Uttar Pradesh due to uniform land quality, cropping pattern and market value of the products. It has been found that the number of fragments of land per capita is higher in many states. The success of any development scheme largely depends on the public support, which helps for its smooth implementation. As the scheme is related with the agrarian development, land records and land management, it invariably needs larger participation of the target groups at various stages of the implementation. The role of grassroots level functionaries and the local bodies is also significant in educating the target beneficiaries in order to extend their co-operation during commissioning of the scheme.

In spite of the slow progress of the scheme in different states, the Government of India still envisages its need for implementation as a progressive measure of land reforms for paving the way for mechanizing agriculture and augmenting its productivity.

End Notes

1. FAO's Report, "The Design of Land Consolidation Pilot Project in Central and Eastern Europe", FAO Corporate Document Repository_files\y4954e06.htm.
2. Mohanty, Bimal K. (1998), "Land Reforms in Orissa", ICSSR Project in Economics, Ravenshaw College, Cuttack, Odisha.
3. Randhawa, M.S. (1947-1981), "A History of Agriculture in India", I.C.A.R., New Delhi, Vol. 14, Chapter 3, p. 27.
4. Rajagopal, Vasant Gumaste; Pingle, Gautam; Bagga, R.K.; Murti, J.R. and Mathur, R.R. (2000), "Study on Review of Performance of Schemes of Consolidation of Land Holdings and Computerization of Land Records", Administrative Staff College of India, Hyderabad, Sponsored by Ministry of Rural Development, Government of India, pp. 152-153.
5. Ibid, p. 160.

7

Institutional Arrangements for Agricultural Credit

Being the backbone of the Indian economy, agriculture has all along been treated as a priority sector for the allocation of institutional credit. The low growth rate of agriculture in the past few years has further strengthened the channels of credit flow to this sector.

Historically, rural co-operative credit institutions (or simply rural co-operatives) have played an important role in providing institutional credit to the agricultural and rural sectors. The structure of rural co-operative banks is not uniform across all the States of the country. Some States have a unitary structure with the State level banks operating through their own branches, while others have a mixed structure incorporating both unitary and federal systems.

Rural indebtedness is noted as a major reason for the spurt in farmer suicides during recent times across a number of states. In most, if not all, such cases, the economic status of the suicide victim was very poor, being small and marginal farmers. After the *green revolution,* agricultural activities have become cash-based individual enterprises requiring high investment in modern inputs and wage labour. This is evident from the list of states with high incidence of farmer suicides, which are not necessarily backward or predominantly agrarian or with low income. Increased liberalization and globalisation have in fact led to a shift in cropping pattern from staple crops to cash crops like oilseeds and cotton, requiring high investment in modern inputs and wage labour, and increasing credit needs but when the prices decline farmers have no means to supplement their incomes.

7.1 Need for Flow of Credit to Agricultural Sector

Agricultural production in India depends upon millions of small farmers. It is the intensity of their effort and the efficiency of their technique that will help in raising yields per acre. Because of inadequate financial resources and absence of timely credit facilities at reasonable rates, many of the farmers, even though otherwise willing, are unable to go in for improved seeds and manures or to introduce better methods or techniques. It is, therefore, of the utmost importance that the financial requirements of the farmers are adequately met.

Provision of sufficient and timely credit at fair rates of interest has, therefore, to be considered as an integral part of agricultural development. Assistance rendered by way of credit has, however, to be related to specific items of productive work or of essential costs of cultivation. Following guidelines from the RBI, commercial banks are increasingly devoting attention to agricultural sector to meet its credit needs.

Agricultural growth is crucial for alleviating rural poverty. Access to institutional credit to more farmers and appropriate quantity and quality of agricultural credit are crucial for realising the full potential of agriculture as a profitable activity.

The Government has taken many policy initiatives for strengthening farm credit delivery system for providing credit at affordable rates of interest to support the resource requirements of the agricultural sector. The emphasis of these initiatives has been on providing timely and adequate credit support to farmers with particular focus on small and marginal farmers and weaker sections of society to enable them to adopt modern technology and improved agricultural practices for increasing agricultural production and productivity. The policy essentially lays emphasis on augmenting credit flow at the ground level through credit planning, adoption of region specific strategies and rationalization of lending policies and procedures and bringing down the rate of interest on farm loan.

7.2 Credit Needs of the Indian Farmers

Need for agricultural credit arises because modern farm technology is costly and the personal resources of the farmers are inadequate. Provision of agricultural credit, as an input, is essential for widespread use of improved agricultural methods.

Credit requirements of the farmers may be classified: (a) on the basis of purpose, and (b) on the basis of time. They need credit for productive as well as for unproductive purposes. Productive purposes include all such activities which help in the improvement of agricultural productivity such as purchase of inputs and permanent improvements in land. Unproductive credit needs include celebration of marriages and other social and religious functions and litigation.

Finance required for productive purposes can be divided broadly into the following categories:

- Short-term (for periods up to 15 months).
- Medium-term (from 15 months up to 5 years).
- Long-term (above 5 years).

Short-term loans are required for purchasing seeds, manures and fertilizers or for meeting labour charges etc. These are expected to be repaid after the harvest.

Medium-term loans are granted for purposes such as sinking of wells, purchase of bullocks, pumping plants and other improved implements etc.

Loans repayable over a longer period (i.e. above 5 years) are classified as long-term loans. These are utilised for payment of old debts, purchase of the heavier machines, making permanent improvements and increasing the size of the holding.

7.3 Sources of Credit for the Farmers

Sources of agricultural credit are grouped into two categories: (a) institutional sources, and (b) non-institutional sources. Institutional sources include co-operative societies, commercial banks and other government agencies. Non-institutional sources comprise moneylenders, landlords, relatives etc.

Till Independence in 1947, money lenders and the

landlords were the principal sources of rural credit. Over the years, the operations of moneylenders have declined in view of debt relief legislations, the system of licensing moneylenders and restrictions on the use and transfer of land as security. Similarly, the abolition of all privileged tenures, both in zamindari and ryotwari areas, has discouraged investment by the landlords and larger cultivators.

7.3.1 Institutional Arrangements: Agricultural credit is disbursed through a multi-agency network comprising of commercial banks, regional rural banks and co-operatives. With their vast network (covering almost all the villages in the country), wider coverage and outreach extending to the remotest part of country, the co-operative credit institutions, both in short and long-term structure are the main institutional mechanism for dispensation of agricultural credit.

7.3.2 Non-institutional Sources: It is true that the institutional sources of credit have weakened the hold of moneylenders on the rural masses. However, the benefits of institutional credit have not percolated to all sections of rural population. Landless workers and marginal farmers have not benefited adequately due to their ignorance of new sources of credit and also on account of their weak repaying capacity. These underprivileged rural sections still depend on the moneylenders and suffer their exploitative practices.

Historically, moneylenders have played a significant role in meeting the credit needs of the rural producers. With stringent laws against money lending and the phenomenal growth of the formal credit delivery system, it was thought that money lenders would soon be out of business. Instead they have been in the business of lending in several disguises.

There are two types of moneylenders in rural areas: (a) agriculturist moneylenders who carry on the business of money lending along with farming, and (b) professional moneylenders whose only occupation is money lending. Although the relative importance of moneylenders has declined over the years, they are still an important source of credit for the rural people, particularly the small farmers and the artisans.

Moneylenders are popular because, unlike government agencies, they give credit for every purpose. They are easily approachable by the credit seekers and there are not many formalities in transacting a loan. However, the malpractices adopted by the moneylenders to exploit the needy farmers cannot be overlooked. These malpractices pertain to charging of high rate of interest and adopting unfair means in the maintenance of accounts.

Agricultural growth is crucial for alleviating rural poverty. Access to institutional credit to more farmers and appropriate quantity and quality of agricultural credit are crucial for realising the full potential of agriculture as a profitable activity.

Provision of sufficient and timely credit at fair rates of interest has, therefore, to be considered as an integral part of agricultural development. Assistance rendered by way of credit has, however, to be related to specific items of productive work or of essential costs of cultivation.

7.4 Co-operative Credit Societies

These societies form an integral part of the rural credit system in India. They are the main source of institutional credit to the farmers. These societies are chiefly responsible for breaking the monopoly of moneylenders in providing credit to the agriculturists. There are around 1 lakh such societies in the country at present. In spite of their suitability and useful role in building up a just socio-economic rural life, co-operative societies suffer from various weaknesses. The heavy overdues of co-operative societies are a cause for concern. The rising overdues have reduced the borrowing and lending activities of these societies. Moreover, these societies have paid inadequate attention to the needs of landless workers and rural artisans. Influential people in the villages have been the main beneficiaries of co-operative credit. Of late, there has been a tendency on the part of political leadership to write-off loans of the farmers. The RBI has repeatedly expressed concern in this regard because non-repayment of loans by the existing borrowers can adversely affect recycling of funds and the credit chances of the prospective borrowers.

7.5 Co-operative Banks

Co-operative banks in India are more than 100 years old. These banks came into existence with the enactment of the Agricultural Credit Co-operative Societies Act in 1904. Co-operative banks form an integral part of the banking system in India. These banks operate mainly for the benefit of rural areas, particularly the agricultural sector. Co-operative banks mobilise deposits and supply agricultural and rural credit with a wider outreach. They are the main source of institutional credit to the farmers. Co-operative banks are chiefly responsible for breaking the monopoly of moneylenders in providing credit to agriculturists. They have also been an important instrument for various development schemes, particularly subsidy-based programmes for the poor. Co-operative banks operate for non-agricultural sector also but their role is small.

Though much smaller as compared to scheduled commercial banks, co-operative banks constitute an important segment of the Indian banking system. They have an extensive branch network and reach out to people in remote areas. They have traditionally played an important role in creating banking habits among the lower and middle-income groups and in strengthening the rural credit delivery system.

The financial reforms process initiated in 1991 has tried to achieve regulatory convergence among various financial intermediaries in view of their systemic importance. Therefore, the basic objectives and instruments of reforms for co-operative banks have been the same as for state co-operative banks (SCBs). However, given the special characteristics of co-operative banks, they have been extended certain dispensations in terms of pace and sequencing of reforms.

7.5.1 Classification of Co-operative Banks: The co-operative banking structure in India comprises urban co-operative banks and rural co-operative credit institutions.

A. Urban Co-operative Banks (UCBs): UCBs consist of a single tier, *viz.* primary co-operative banks, commonly referred to as urban co-operative banks.

B. Rural Co-operatives: Based on the nature of their lending operations, rural credit co-operatives have traditionally been bifurcated into two parallel wings: short-term and long-term.

7.6 Rural Co-operatives

7.6.1 Short-term Rural Co-operatives: The short-term provide crop and other working capital loans to farmers and rural artisans primarily for short-term purposes. These credit institutions have a three-tier federal structure. (a) At the apex of the system is a state co-operative bank (SCB) in each State. (b) At the middle (or district) level, there are central co-operative banks (CCBs) also known as district co-operative banks. (c) At the lowest (or village) level are the primary agricultural credit societies (PACS). The smaller States and Union Territories (UTs) have a two-tier structure with SCBs directly meeting the credit requirements of PACS.

A. State Co-operative Bank (SCB): SCB is the highest agency of the three-tier co-operative credit structure in a state. It serves as a link between RBI and the CCBs and PACS. The RBI provides credit to lower level co-operatives through the SCB. This function of the RBI has now been taken over by NABARD. The SCB also acts as a *balancing centre* for CCBs in the sense that surplus funds of some CCBs are made available to other needy CCBs. The SCB exercises general control and supervision over CCBs and PACS.

B. Central Co-operative Banks (CCBs): These banks act as a link between the SCB and the PACS. The main task of CCBs is to lend money to affiliated village primary societies. The CCBs are expected to attract deposits from the general public.

C. Primary Agricultural Credit Societies (PACS): These societies form the basic unit of the co-operative credit system in India. These voluntary societies based on the principle of one man one vote have posed challenge to the exploitative practices of the village moneylenders.

The farmers and other small-time borrowers come in direct contact with these societies. The success of the co-operative credit movement depends largely on the strength of these village level societies. There are more than 93,000 such societies in the country at present.

As a result of the expansion of the activities of PACS, the role of moneylenders in providing credit to agriculturists has decreased over the years. A major objective of PACS is to serve the needs of weaker sections of the society. For this purpose, the people with limited means, particularly scheduled castes and scheduled tribes, are encouraged to become members of these societies. Government has promoted multi-purpose societies in tribal areas for the benefit of people living there.

7.6.2 Long-term Rural Co-operatives: The long-term provide typically medium and long-term loans for making investments in agriculture, rural industries and, in the recent period, housing. Generally, these co-operatives have two tiers, *viz.*

- **State Co-operative Agriculture and Rural Development Banks (SCARDBs):** These banks operate at the State level.
- **Primary Co-operative Agriculture and Rural Development Banks (PCARDBs):** These banks operate at the *taluka/tehsil* level.

7.7 Rural Co-operatives: History and Recent Policy Measures

Rural credit co-operatives in India were originally envisaged as a mechanism for pooling the resources of people with small means and providing them with access to different financial services. Democratic in features, the movement was also an effective instrument for development of degraded waste lands, increasing productivity, providing food security, generating employment opportunities in rural areas and ensuring social and economic justice to the poor and vulnerable.

The history of the co-operative credit movement in India can be traced back to 1904 when the Co-operative Societies Act was passed. In 1919, *co-operation* became a provincial subject. The Co-operative Planning Committee, 1945 found that a large number of co-operatives were "saddled with the problem of frozen assets because of heavy overdues in repayment".

The co-operative banks in India play an important role in catering to the banking needs of the rural population. Soon after Independence in 1947, the inadequacy of rural credit engaged the attention of the Government of India and the RBI. The agricultural credit system as it has emerged over the years is the result of both evolution and intervention, and symbolises the nation's response to the dissatisfaction with the discredited colonial credit delivery system.

The Reserve Bank of India Act, 1934 has specific provisions relating to agricultural credit. Section 54 of the RBI Act specifically authorised the creation of an Agricultural Credit Department within the RBI to deal not only with the rural credit but also with the long-term finance including refinance. Section 17 of the Act empowered it to provide agricultural credit through state co-operative banks or any other banks engaged in the business of agricultural credit.

The foundation for building a broader credit infrastructure for rural credit was laid down by the All India Rural Credit Survey (1954). The Committee of Direction that conducted the survey recommended the creation of National Agricultural Credit Fund, which was subsequently created by the RBI. The Agricultural Refinance Corporation (ARC) set up by the RBI in 1963 provided funds by way of refinance, but credit co-operatives still did not function too well. Decentralised credit planning through the Lead

Bank Scheme was also introduced to spearhead the credit allocation for, *inter alia*, agricultural lending. In order to emphasise the developmental and promotional role assigned to the ARC in addition to refinancing, the ARC was renamed as the Agricultural Refinance and Development Corporation (ARDC) in 1975.

Despite all these efforts, the flow of credit to the agricultural sector failed to exhibit any appreciable improvement as the co-operatives lacked resources to meet the expected demand. To solve these problems, the regional rural banks (RRBs) were set up in 1975. In order to strengthen the institutional credit for agriculture and rural development, National Bank for Agriculture and Rural Development (NABARD) was set up on July 12, 1982. On its establishment, NABARD took over the entire functions of the ARDC, the refinancing functions of the RBI in relation to co-operatives and regional rural banks (RRBs).

The rural credit co-operative system has served as an important instrument of credit delivery in rural and agricultural areas. The separate structure of rural co-operative sector for long-term and short-term loans has enabled these institutions to develop as specialised institutions for rural credit delivery. At the same time, their federal structure has helped in providing support structure for the guidance and critical financing for the lower structure. These institutions have wide outreach with as many as 93,413 primary agricultural co-operative societies (PACS), the grass root organisation of the rural co-operative banking structure with over 9 crore members, operating in the country as on March 31, 2013.

The rural co-operative credit institutions, however, are beset with many problems which include the following.

1. Low resource base.
2. High dependence on refinancing agencies.
3. Lack of diversification.
4. Huge accumulated losses.
5. Persistent NPAs.

6. Low recovery levels.
7. Various other types of organisational weaknesses.

NABARD and the RBI, therefore, have been taking several supervisory and developmental measures in consultation with the Government of India for the revival of weak institutions and orderly growth of this important segment of the financial sector.

7.8 Primary Agricultural Credit Societies (PACS)

Primary agricultural credit societies (PACS) are the foundation of the co-operative credit system on which the superstructure of the short-term co-operative credit system rests. It is the PACS which directly interface with individual farmers, provide short-term and medium-term credit, supply agricultural inputs, distribute consumer articles and arrange for marketing of produce of its members through a co-operative marketing society.

PACS continue to rely heavily on external support and have not yet been able to become self-reliant in respect of resources through deposit mobilisation and internal accruals, affecting their growth and expansion of business activities.

PACS need to function as viable units responsive to the needs, aspirations and convenience of its members, particularly those belonging to the more vulnerable sections of the society. They must function effectively as well-managed and multi-purpose institutions mobilising the savings of the rural people and providing a package of services including credit, supply of agricultural inputs and implements, consumer goods, marketing services and technical guidance with focus on weaker sections.

Some of the critical challenges facing primary level co-operative credit institutions, apart from improving resource mobilisation, are the following.

1. Increasing diversification in business portfolio.
2. Improving volume of business.
3. Arresting decline in membership by the borrowers.

4. Reducing cost of management.
5. Correcting imbalances in loans outstanding.
6. Improving skills of staff and imparting professionalisation.
7. Strengthening management information system (MIS).
8. Reducing involvement in non/less profitable business.

7.9 Problems of Rural Co-operatives

Rural co-operatives form an integral part of the rural credit system in India. They are the main source of institutional credit to the farmers. These societies are chiefly responsible for breaking the monopoly of moneylenders in providing credit to the agriculturists.

Despite the phenomenal outreach and volume of operations, the financial health of a very large proportion of rural credit co-operatives has deteriorated significantly. The institutions are beset with problems like low resource base, high dependence on external sources of funding, excessive governmental control, dual control, huge accumulated losses, imbalances, poor business diversification, low recovery etc.

These institutions do not, therefore, inspire confidence among their existing and potential members, depositors, borrowers and lenders.

Thus, there is a need to find ways for strengthening the co-operative movement and making it a well-managed and vibrant medium to serve the credit needs of rural India, especially the small and marginal farmers.

Moreover, these societies have paid inadequate attention to the needs of landless workers and rural artisans. Influential people in the villages have been the main beneficiaries of co-operative credit. Of late, there has been a tendency on the part of political leadership to write-off loans of the farmers. The RBI has repeatedly expressed concern in this regard because non-repayment of loans by the existing borrowers can adversely affect recycling of funds and the credit chances of the prospective borrowers. A national approach on this issue is required so that co-operative credit system may fulfil the task assigned to it.

It is part of a historic policy infirmity which allowed co-operatives to be treated as *refinance windows* instead of incentivising them into becoming genuine thrift and credit institutions.

The rural co-operative credit institutions are beset with many problems which include the following:

1. Low resource base.
2. High dependence on refinancing agencies.
3. Lack of diversification.
4. Huge accumulated losses.
5. Persistent non-performing assets (NPAs).
6. Low recovery levels.
7. Various other types of organisational weaknesses.

NABARD and the RBI, therefore, have been taking several supervisory and developmental measures in consultation with the Government of India for the revival of weak institutions and orderly growth of this important segment of the financial sector.

7.10 NABARD and the Co-operative Sector

National Bank for Agriculture and Rural Development (NABARD) provides refinance to state co-operative agriculture and rural development banks (SCARDBs), state co-operative banks (SCBs), regional rural banks (RRBs) and other financial institutions approved by the RBI. The ultimate beneficiaries of refinance from NABARD could be individuals, partnership concerns, companies, State-owned corporations or co-operative societies.

7.10.1 Credit Extended by NABARD: NABARD provides short-term credit facilities to SCBs in respect of eligible CCBs for the following purposes:

1. Financing seasonal agricultural operations.
2. Marketing of crops.
3. Pisciculture activities.
4. Production and marketing activities of primary weavers/other industrial co-operative societies.
5. Labour contract/forest labour co-operative societies.

6. Individual rural artisans through PCS.
7. Procurement, stocking and distribution of chemical fertilisers.
8. Approved agricultural, allied and other marketing activities.

Besides short-term credit limits are also sanctioned to SCBs on behalf of apex/regional weavers/other industrial societies for financing procurement and marketing and trading-in-yarn.

Short-term limits are also provided to RRBs for financing seasonal agricultural operations, marketing of crops and pisciculture activities.

Medium-term facilities are also provided to SCBs and RRBs for converting short-term into medium-term loans and for approved agricultural investments.

Long-term loans are provided to the State Governments for contributing to the share capital of co-operative credit institutions.

7.11 Agricultural Credit: Recent Policy Announcements

Concerned over the slower growth of agriculture credit, the Government announced a comprehensive policy on June 18, 2004. The policy envisaged a 30 percent increase in credit to agriculture sector in 2004-05 over an estimated credit flow of ₹ 80,000 crore in 2003-04. The implementation of the policy was entrusted to public sector banks, private sector banks, regional rural banks (RRBs) and co-operative banks. The policy indicated that each rural and semi-urban branch of commercial banks, on an average, would take up at least two to three new investment projects in the area of plantation and horticulture, fisheries, organic farming, agro-processing, livestock, micro irrigation, sprinkler irrigation, watershed management, village pond development and other agricultural activities. NABARD was asked to advise District Level Technical Committees to review the scales of finance to meet the realistic credit needs of farmers, especially for capital intensive agricultural operations.

The Budget for 2004-05, presented in the Parliament on July 8, 2004, proposed doubling of credit to agriculture in three years and announced further measures to achieve the target growth in agricultural credit.

These measures included holding the sponsor bank of each RRB squarely responsible for the performance of RRB under its control and an incentive scheme under which RRBs, adopting new governance standards and abiding by prudential regulations, qualified for receiving funds from the Government for their restructuring.

The Budget proposed setting up of a Task Force to examine the reforms required in the co-operative banking system including the appropriate regulatory regime.

Consequent upon above mentioned policy measures, the flow of institutional credit to the agricultural sector has increased significantly in recent years (Table 7.1).

Table 7.1: Flow of Institutional Credit to Agriculture and Allied Activities

(₹ crore)

Agency	2008-09	2009-10	2010-11	2011-12^	2012-13*
Co-operative Banks	46,192 (15)	63,497 (17)	78,121 (17)	87,963 (17)	64,664 (27)
Regional Rural Banks	26,765 (9)	35,218 (9)	44,293 (10)	54,450 (11)	32,127 (13)
Commercial Banks	2,28,951 (76)	2,85,799 (74)	3,45,877 (74)	3,68,616 (72)	1,42,838 (60)
Total	3,01,908	3,84,514	4,68,291	5,11,029	2,39,629

^ Provisional; * Up to September 2012

Figures in parentheses indicate percentage of total flow of institutional credit.

Source: Government of India, *Economic Survey*, 2012-13, p. 111, Table 5.7.

7.11.1 Agricultural Debt Waiver and Debt Relief Scheme, 2008: In the wake of suicides by farmers in some parts of the country, indebtedness of the farmers was high on the agenda of the Government. The Government had appointed a Committee (Chairman: R. Radhakrishna) to examine all aspects of agricultural indebtedness. The Committee in its report made a number of recommendations but stopped short of recommending waiver of agricultural loans. However,

Government was conscious of the problems being faced by the farmers, especially the small and marginal farmers. Having carefully weighed the pros and cons of debt waiver and having taken into account the resource position, the Finance Minister announced the following scheme of debt waiver and debt relief for farmers:

1. All agricultural loans disbursed by scheduled commercial banks, regional rural banks and co-operative credit institutions up to March 31, 2007 and overdue as on December 31, 2007 were covered under the scheme.
2. For marginal farmers (i.e., holding up to 1 hectare) and small farmers (1-2 hectare), there was a complete waiver of all loans that were overdue on December 31, 2007 and which remained unpaid until February 29, 2008. In respect of other farmers, there was a one time settlement (OTS) scheme for all loans that were overdue on December 31, 2007 and which remained unpaid until February 29, 2008. Under the OTS, a rebate of 25 percent was given against payment of the balance of 75 percent.
3. Agricultural loans were restructured and rescheduled by banks in 2004 and 2006 through special packages. These rescheduled loans, and other loans rescheduled in the normal course as per RBI guidelines, were also eligible either for a waiver or an OTS on the same pattern.
4. The implementation of the debt waiver and debt relief scheme was to be completed by June 30, 2008. Upon being granted debt waiver or signing an agreement for debt relief under the OTS, the farmer was entitled to fresh agricultural loans from the banks in accordance with normal rules.
5. Government estimated that about 3 crore small and marginal farmers and about 1 crore other farmers would benefit from the scheme. The total value of overdue loans waived was estimated at ₹ 50,000 crore and the OTS relief on the overdue loans at ₹ 10,000 crore.

In addition to above, Government has initiated several

measures to galvanize the institutional credit system to make it more responsive to the needs of farmers. Some of the important measures initiated in this regard are as under:

1. Banks have been advised to simplify procedures for documentation for agricultural loans.
2. As part of the measures announced by the RBI for financial inclusion, banks have been advised to open *no frills* accounts and issue simple overdraft facility against such accounts. Banks have also been advised to issue General Credit Cards up to ₹ 25,000 without insisting on security and end use of funds.
3. Banks have been advised to undertake, on a pilot basis, 100 percent financial inclusion in at least one district in each State. Based on the success of the pilot, the State Level Bankers Committee in the States will draw a time-bound plan for achieving 100 percent financial inclusion in other districts of the State.

To sum up, in spite of their suitability and useful role in building up a just socio-economic rural life, co-operative societies suffer from various weaknesses and their performance has been far from satisfactory in certain respects. The heavy overdues of co-operative societies are a cause for concern. The rising overdues have reduced the borrowing and lending activities of these societies. The increasing incidence of defaulting has brought bad name to these societies.

Co-operative societies have paid inadequate attention to the needs of landless workers and the rural artisans. The influential people in the villages have been the main beneficiaries of co-operative credit. Of late, there has been a tendency on the part of political leadership to write off the loans of the farmers. The RBI has repeatedly expressed concern in this regard because the non-repayment of loans by the existing borrowers adversely affects recycling of funds and the credit chances of prospective borrowers. A national approach on this issue is required so that co-operative credit system may fulfil the task assigned to it.

Positive impact of reforms, as has been witnessed in the case of commercial banking sector, may take longer to get manifested for co-operative banks given the late start of the reform process in this sector. Unless such a positive scenario evolves for the co-operative banking sector in the near future, the financial health of many of these banks would continue to remain a cause of concern.

It is imperative that the government takes initiatives to expand the network of institutional credit facilities in the rural areas and that the credit needs of the small and marginal farmers are met through earmarking credit for the group. Extension and marketing initiatives need to focus on this segment. At the same time, group initiatives need to be encouraged and awareness among the group has to be increased. The procedural formalities also have to be made less stringent to make the system more user-friendly for the largely illiterate group.

Given the distress among the farmers, it is important that a safety-net programme is introduced to ensure a minimum income for the farmers. Also the risk factor has to be mitigated through adequate insurance and credit facilities. At the same time, the outreach and efficiency of the institutional credit sources have to be improved. This is important to protect the small and marginal farmers who still heavily rely on private moneylenders who charge high interest rates and follow unscrupulous means to perpetuate indebtedness.

8

Agricultural Marketing: System and Reforms

During the pre-Independence period, Indian agriculture was backward and stagnant and there was hardly any marketable surplus. Therefore, the system of marketing, though defective, did not attract much attention. However, in the post-Independence period and particularly after the green revolution, agricultural marketing has become a prime concern for the planners. Due to increase in agricultural productivity, the marketable surplus has increased, necessitating reforms in the existing system. The objectives of these reforms are to ensure: (a) fair prices for the produce of the farmers, (b) adequate and regular availability of foodgrains for urban areas, and (c) regular supplies of raw materials for the industries.

Sale of agricultural produce involves a number of functions such as assembling, storing, grading, standardising, transporting and financing the produce and negotiating sale. Some of these operations may be performed by the farmer, but storage and sale of a commodity and finding finance for purchase, call for specialised knowledge and adequate resources which the individual cultivator does not possess.

8.1 Importance of Agricultural Marketing

Marketing is the last link in the chain of production process. An efficient marketing system which ensures reasonable return to the producers is essential to induce them to produce more. Disposal of the produce after harvest and the return obtained have a significant effect on production and on the welfare of the cultivator. Production in agriculture being seasonal, the crop is harvested during a short period and consumed gradually.

While commodities like cotton and groundnut require large storage space which the average cultivator lacks, fruits, vegetables and sugarcane are of a perishable nature. The farmer has, therefore, to dispose of his surplus immediately either at the village or at the *mandi.* In the absence of staying power of a large number of small farmers, they compete with each other and the markets witness conditions of occasional glut and scarcity. A major part of the commercial crops like cotton, jute, sugarcane and oilseeds has to be marketed immediately as the farmers are in need of cash for meeting their dues and other expenses. As regards foodgrains the marketable surplus varies by crops and regions. The total quantity and value of the marketed produce, even in a predominantly subsistence economy as in India is considerable.

The village money lender or the *mandi arhatiya* advances loans to farmers for securing production requirements like seeds, and manures and for meeting other needs. These debts some times carry an understanding or an obligation to sell the produce to or through the lender or his nominee. At the time of sale the position of advantage occupied by the village banker gets reflected either in a lower price or unfair weights or delayed settlement. If the sale takes place in the *mandi* or the market through the brokers or *arhatiyas* the farmer pays not only for the services rendered by the middlemen but is also subjected to other unwarranted deductions.

The benefits of a regulated market which attempt only to improve the existing practices are limited. Without changing the marketing structure the number of middlemen and costs cannot be reduced. Efforts in this direction have been made in some States by organising co-operative marketing. The progress of marketing societies, in spite of immense scope, has so far been slow. The entry of a co-operative even as an agent is not generally favoured by the trade.

8.2 Present Practices of Marketing Agricultural Produce

Various systems of agricultural marketing exist in India.

An important traditional system is the sale of produce to moneylenders and village traders. This system is closely related to the problem of rural indebtedness. Farmers who are indebted to moneylenders are forced to sell their produce to them. It is understandable that the price paid by the moneylenders is considerably lower than the market price.

Another traditional practice is the sale of produce in the *hats* and *shandies*. *Hats* are village markets held once or twice a week and serve a small cluster of villages. *Shandies* are also village markets held at longer intervals or on special occasions.

An important component of the marketing system is the widespread network of regulated wholesale markets. These markets are generally located near or in a township and serve a number of surrounding villages. The farmers sell their produce to the commission agents with the help of brokers. It is well-known that various types of malpractices exist in these markets, e.g. use of wrong measures and weights. *Hats* and *shandies* constitute, for a great majority of farmers in India, particularly the small producers, the focal points for disposal of farm produce as well as sale and purchase centres for non-agricultural products.

Involvement of government agencies with the marketing of agricultural produce is a welcome development. Co-operative societies and government agencies have helped the farmers to escape the exploitative practices of the private dealers. Leading agencies involved in procurement and support price operations on behalf of the Government are: Food Corporation of India, Cotton Corporation of India, Jute Corporation of India and the Co-operatives with National Agricultural Co-operative Marketing Federation (NAFED) as their apex organisation.

From time to time, Government announces procurement or minimum support prices for various agricultural crops.

8.3 Marketing Organizations of the Ministry of Agriculture

The Government has been playing an important role in

developing the agricultural marketing system in the country. Department of Agriculture and Cooperation in the Ministry of Agriculture, Government of India, has 3 organizations dealing with marketing under its administrative control, namely Directorate of Marketing and Inspection (DMI) Faridabad, Chaudhary Charan Singh National Institute of Agricultural Marketing (NIAM), Jaipur and Small Farmers Agri-business Consortium (SFAC), New Delhi.

8.3.1 Directorate of Marketing and Inspection (DMI): DMI is an attached office of the Ministry of Agriculture. It was set up in 1935 to implement the agricultural marketing policies and programmes of the Central Government. Since its inception, the Directorate continues to be responsible for bringing about an integrated development of marketing of agricultural and allied produce in the country with a view to safeguarding the interests of producer-sellers as well as the consumers. It maintains a close liaison between the Central and the State Governments in the implementation of agricultural marketing policies in the country.

The main functions of the DMI are the following:

1. Promotion of standardization and grading of agricultural and allied produce under the Agricultural Produce (Grading and Marking) Act, 1937 as amended in 1986.
2. Training of personnel in agricultural marketing.
3. Advising State Governments on regulation and management of agricultural produce markets.
4. Marketing extension.
5. Agricultural marketing information network.
6. Construction of rural godowns.
7. Development of agricultural marketing infrastructure, grading and standardization.

The activities of the DMI cover the following areas of agricultural marketing:

1. **Standardization and Grading:** The Agricultural Produce (Grading and Marking) Act, 1937 provides for grading and marking of agricultural and other produce. The Act

empowers the Central Government to make Rules for: (a) fixing grade designation to indicate quality of any scheduled article, (b) defining the quality indicated by every grade designation, and (c) specifying grade designation marks to represent particular grade designations. Standards notified as per the provisions of the Act are popularly called AGMARK Standards. These standards differentiate between quality and 2-3 grades are prescribed for each commodity. Grades help farmers/traders to get prices for agricultural commodities as per the quality produced by them and consumers get the desired quality. Till date, grade standards for 203 agricultural commodities have been notified. These include fruits and vegetables, cereals, pulses, oilseeds, vegetable oils, ghee, spices, honey, creamery butter, wheat atta, besan etc. These commodities can also be certified under AGMARK as per the prescribed grade standards. Vegetable oils, spices, ghee, creamery butter, honey, wheat atta, besan etc. are popularly certified under AGMARK. Grading and marking of agricultural commodities is voluntary as per the provisions of the Act.

2. **Regulation, Development and Management of Agricultural Produce Markets:** Agricultural markets are regulated and managed under the Agricultural Produce Marketing (Regulation) Acts enacted by the respective State Governments. The Central Government provides guidance and assistance in regulation and development of agricultural produce markets. By the end of March, 2010, 7,157 markets have been brought under the ambit of regulation. In the perspective of agricultural marketing reforms, DMI prepared the Model APMC Act, 2003 and the Model APMC Rules, 2007 and circulated them to all the State Governments/UT Administrations for consideration and adoption.
3. **Marketing Research and Information Network (AGMARKNET):** This Central sector scheme was launched by the Ministry of Agriculture, Government of India, in March 2000. The market information network,

AGMARKNET is being implemented jointly by DMI and NIC, using NICNET facilities available throughout the country. The objective of the scheme is to facilitate collection and dissemination of information for better price realization by the farmers. The information covers market-related, price-related, infrastructure-related and promotion-related issues for efficient marketing.

4. **Construction of Rural Godowns:** A network of rural godowns enables small farmers to avoid distress sale by enhancing their holding capacity and sell their produce at remunerative prices. Accordingly, DMI launched Grameen Bhandaran Yojana w.e.f. April 1, 2001. The main objectives of the scheme include creation of scientific storage capacity with allied facilities in rural areas to meet various requirements of farmers for storing farm produce, processed farm produce, agricultural inputs etc. and help them to avoid distress sale by creating the facility of pledge loan and marketing credit.
5. **Marketing Reforms:** The State Governments have been advised suitably to modify APMC Act to facilitate: (a) development of competitive markets in private and cooperative sectors, (b) allow procurement of agricultural commodities directly from farmers fields, and (c) to establish effective linkage between the farm production and the retail chain and food processing industries. In the wake of the economic liberalization, the concept of contract farming in which national and multi-national companies enter into contracts for marketing of agricultural produce and to provide technology and capital to farmers has gained importance. These arrangements have to be promoted as an effective method of linking small farmers to sources of extension, advice, mechanization, seeds and credit and to assured and profitable markets.
6. **Modern Terminal Market Complex:** In order to harness the potential of emerging consumer demand for horticulture commodities, a professionally managed competitive alternate

marketing structure which provides multiple choices to farmers for sale along with a comprehensive solution to meet key needs of the stakeholders is necessary. Such a system entails high investment cost and development of efficient skills, each of which can be infused by inviting private sector participation in the sector. Thus, the modern terminal market in hub and spoke model was conceptualized to be set up on a public private partnership basis with the objective of fulfilling the above goals. The scheme is being implemented through a subsidy route under National Horticulture Mission with active involvement of all stakeholders at various levels under public private partnership mode.

8.3.2 Chaudhary Charan Singh National Institute of Agricultural Marketing (NIAM): NIAM is a premier national level institute set up by the Government of India in August 1988 to offer specialized training, research, education and consultancy in the field of agricultural marketing. NIAM is an autonomous body under the aegis of the Ministry of Agriculture, Government of India. It was set up as a registered society to cater to the needs of agricultural marketing personnel in India as well as from South East Asian Countries.

NIAM offers a two year post-graduate diploma in agri-business management programme (PGDABM) which is an AICTE approved residential programme, for students with undergraduate degree in agriculture and allied sciences. The programme combines the best of MBA with unique skills required for a career in agri-business.

8.3.3 Small Farmers' Agri-Business Consortium (SFAC): SFAC was registered by Ministry of Agriculture, Government of India on January 18, 1994 as a society under the Societies Registration Act, 1860. Currently, the members include RBI, SBI, IDBI, EXIM Bank, Oriental Bank of Commerce, NABARD, Canara Bank, NAFED, United Phosphorous Ltd. etc. The mission of the society is to support innovative ideas for generating income and employment in rural areas by promoting private investment in agri-business projects.

The Central sector scheme for agri-business development is being implemented by SFAC in close association with commercial banks for providing: (a) venture capital to agri-business projects, and (b) assistance to farmers/producers' groups for preparing quality detailed project reports (DPR).

For effective implementation of the scheme, SFAC has already signed MoU with 21 commercial banks.

8.4 Inter-Ministerial Task Force on Agricultural Marketing

The Inter-Ministerial Task Force set up by the Ministry of Agriculture to strengthen and develop agricultural marketing submitted its Report in June 2002, outlining several reforms in agricultural marketing. It recommended amendment to the States' Agricultural Produce Marketing Acts for promotion of direct marketing and contract farming, development of agricultural markets in private and cooperative sectors, stepping up of pledge financing, expansion of futures trading to cover all agricultural commodities, introduction of negotiable warehousing receipt system and use of information technology to provide market led extension services to farmers. At a National Conference on Agriculture Marketing Reforms organized by the Ministry of Agriculture on 27th September 2002 in New Delhi, all the State Governments and Union Territory Administrations were requested to implement the reforms measures by bringing out suitable amendments in the existing state legislation. A Committee of State Ministers has also been set up under the Chairmanship of Union Minister of State (Agriculture) to accelerate the implementation of the reform measures.

8.5 Salient Features of the Model Act for State Agricultural Produce Marketing (Development and Regulation) Act, 2003

Marketing of agricultural produce is the most important activity for the farming community, particularly for those who are small producers and have small surpluses for marketing. To protect the interests of farmers, Government promoted organized marketing of agricultural commodities through a network of regulated markets. However, studies indicate that the institutions of regulated markets have achieved limited success, as these markets restricted development of direct and free marketing, smooth raw material supplied to agro-processors, information exchange and adoption of innovative marketing systems and technologies.

To benefit the farming community from new market access opportunities, the internal agricultural marketing system in the country needs to be integrated and strengthened. In this context, an inter-Ministerial Task Force set up by the Ministry of Agriculture suggested a package of reform measures, such as amendments in the States' Agricultural Produce Marketing Acts to encourage development of competitive agricultural markets in the private and cooperative sectors, and deregulation of marketing system to promote private investment in marketing infrastructure.

The Department of Agriculture and Cooperation has formulated a model law on agricultural marketing and contract farming in consultation with the State Governments and representatives of trade and industry. The salient features of the model law are given below:

1. Legal persons, growers and local authorities permitted to establish new markets in any area.
2. No compulsion on growers to sell their produce through existing regulated markets.
3. Establishment of direct purchase centres, consumers/farmers markets for direct sale.
4. Promotion of public-private partnership in the management and development of agricultural markets.
5. Separate constitution of special markets for commodities like onions, fruits, vegetables, and flowers.
6. A separate chapter to regulate and promote contract-farming arrangements in the country.
7. Prohibition of commission agency in any transaction of agricultural commodities with the producers.

8. Market Committee to promote alternative marketing system, contract farming, direct marketing and farmers/consumers markets.
9. State Marketing Boards to promote standardization, grading, quality certification, market led extension and training of farmers and market functionaries in marketing related areas.
10. Constitution of State Marketing Standards Bureau for promotion of grading, standardization and quality certification of agricultural produce.

The Government of Karnataka has taken initiative in this direction and inserted a new Chapter (Chapter XIII A) in the Karnataka Agricultural Produce Marketing (Regulation) Act, 1910, to provide for the establishment of an Integrated Produce Market to be owned and managed by the National Dairy Development Board (NDDB) for marketing of fruits, vegetables and flowers in that State. Other States also need to amend respective Agricultural Produce Marketing Acts to permit any organization or corporate body to establish integrated facility for marketing of agricultural produce. Curtailment of excessive bureaucratization of markets is necessary for healthy growth of such markets.

Liberalization of world trade in agriculture has provided new opportunities to the farm sector to access markets for agricultural commodities world-wide. However, to make this happen, reforms have to be brought about in agriculture sector to remove all barriers, whether legal or policy induced, which introduce inefficiencies and monopoly rents in the functioning of agricultural markets. At present, though agricultural production is largely free from controls, the same is not true of marketing of agricultural commodities. Under the APMC Act, State Governments alone are empowered to initiate the process of setting up of markets for agriculture products within a defined area. As a result private and co-operative sectors cannot take initiative in setting up markets equipped with more modern facilities.

High investments together with entrepreneurial skills

required for creation and managing the market infrastructures have to come from private sector in order to encourage private sector participation and investments required for development of alternative marketing infrastructure and supporting services, provisions of the State Agricultural Produce Marketing Regulation Act would need modification to create a lawful role for the private sector in market development. Government's role should be that of a facilitator rather than that of exercising control over the management of markets.

8.6 Agricultural Marketing and Trade in the National Policy for Farmers

The National Policy for Farmers announced by the Government in 2007 envisaged various measures to improve marketing and trade practices related to agricultural produce. It observed, "Assured and remunerative marketing opportunities hold the key to continued progress in enhancing farm productivity and profitability. Several significant market reforms have already been initiated by the Central and the State governments. These reforms provide more options to farmers for selling their produce, allowing the private sector, including cooperatives, to develop markets, promote direct sales to consumers, processors and retail chain suppliers/exporters and remove scope for corruption and harassment. The following steps would be taken:

- The minimum support price (MSP) mechanism would be implemented effectively across the country.
- The Market Intervention Scheme (MIS) would be strengthened to respond speedily to exigencies especially in the case of sensitive crops in the rain-fed areas.
- The establishment of community foodgrains banks would be promoted to help in the marketing of underutilised crops and thereby generate an economic stake in the conservation of agro-biodiversity.
- The food security basket will be enlarged by storing and selling nutritious millets such as bajra, jowar and ragi and other crops through the network of the public distribution

system (PDS).

- Efforts will be made to develop a single national market by relaxing internal restrictions. All controls and regulations hindering increase in farmers' income will be reviewed and abolished.
- Terminal markets for agriculture would be developed in public-private partnership mode to provide better market access to farmers with better price realisation in a transparent trading environment with suitable backward linkages to give technical backstopping services needed for quality and demand driven production.
- The role of the Agriculture Produce Market Committees and State Agriculture Marketing Boards would be transformed from mere regulatory focus to promotion of grading, branding, packaging and development of markets for local produce.

Farmers require authentic advice based on meteorological, marketing and management information for land-use decisions and investments. Infrastructure support would be put in place to minimise post-harvest losses and enable agro-processing and value-addition at the village level itself to increase employment and income. Farmers' organisations and other entities like cooperatives and small farmers' estates would be encouraged so that farmers can get a fair deal and enjoy the economies of scale. Producer groups and co-operatives will be encouraged to promote agro-processing industry. Constraints would be removed for improving the negotiability of warehouse receipts.

The trade policies in agriculture would aim at protecting the livelihood of farmer families and fostering their economic well-being. Effective livelihood security for farmers would be put in place. Quality and trade literacy programmes would be launched across the country. Appropriate measures would be introduced to mitigate price risks and enable the stakeholders, particularly the farmers, to hedge their risk.

Farmers' associations and SHGs would be supported to

export on competitive terms by spreading awareness of the opportunities available for external agricultural trade and for value addition. The agri-export zones would be further strengthened to become places where farmers will get the best possible price for their produce.

The twin goals of ensuring justice to farmers in terms of a remunerative price for their produce and to consumers in terms of a fair and affordable price for staples (as farmers are also consumers) would be achieved through the following integrated strategy:

- The government, while taking decisions on MSP, would ensure that the farmers' interests in receiving remunerative prices for their produce are adequately safeguarded.
- Stable and efficient market environment, including effective implementation of MSP in rain-fed areas, would add to the improvement in productivity and income in dry land farming.

Terms of reference and status of the Commission for Agricultural Costs and Prices (CACP) would be reviewed to make the MSP regime more effective". [1]

8.7 Gramin Bhandaran Yojana (Rural Godown Scheme)

It is well known that the small farmers do not have the economic strength to retain the produce with them till the market prices are favourable. There has been a felt need in the country to provide the farming community with facilities for scientific storage so that wastage and produce deterioration are avoided and also to enable it to meet its credit requirement without being compelled to sell the produce at a time when the prices are low. A network of rural godowns will enable small farmers to enhance their holding capacity in order to sell their produce at remunerative prices and avoid distress sales.

Accordingly, Grameen Bhandaran Yojana, a Capital Investment Subsidy Scheme for Construction/Renovation of Rural Godowns was introduced in 2001-2002 and extended up to 31.03.2007. The Scheme was extended for implementation during the period of the Eleventh Five Year Plan (2007-12), with modifications in its operational guidelines for new projects to be sanctioned after June 26, 2008.

8.7.1 Objectives of the Scheme: The main objectives of the scheme include the following:

1. Creation of scientific storage capacity with allied facilities in rural areas to meet the requirements of farmers for storing farm produce, processed farm produce and agricultural inputs.
2. Promotion of grading, standardization and quality control of agricultural produce to improve their marketability.
3. Prevention of distress sale immediately after harvest by providing the facility of pledge financing and marketing credit.
4. Strengthen agricultural marketing infrastructure in the country by paving the way for the introduction of a national system of warehouse receipts in respect of agricultural commodities stored in such godowns.
5. To reverse the declining trend of investment in agriculture sector by encouraging private and cooperative sectors to invest in the creation of storage infrastructure in the country.

8.7.2 Salient Features of the Scheme: These are the following:

1. Projects for construction of rural godowns can be taken up by individuals, farmers, group of farmers/growers, partnership and proprietary firms, non-government organizations (NGOs), self-help groups (SHGs), companies, corporations, co-operatives, local bodies other than municipal corporations, federations, agricultural produce marketing committees, marketing boards and agro-processing corporations in the entire country. Assistance for renovation of rural godowns is restricted to godowns constructed by co-operatives only.
2. Under the scheme, the entrepreneur is free to construct godown at any place, as per his/her commercial judgment except for the restriction that it would be outside the limits

of municipal corporation area. Rural godowns constructed in the food parks promoted by the Ministry of Food Processing Industries are also eligible under the scheme for assistance.

3. Capacity of a godown is decided by an entrepreneur. However, subsidy under the scheme is restricted to a minimum capacity of 100 tonnes and maximum capacity of 10,000 tonnes. However, there is no maximum ceiling on subsidy in the case of projects of rural godowns of cooperatives assisted by NCDC.
4. Rural godowns of smaller sizes up to 50 tonnes capacity are also eligible for subsidy under the scheme as a special case based on viability analysis depending on the topography/special requirement of the State/Region. In hilly areas (where the project site is located at a height of more than 1,000 meters above mean sea level), rural godowns of smaller size up to 25 tonnes capacity will also be eligible for subsidy.

8.8 Agricultural Marketing Information Network (AGMARKNET), 2000

Market information is needed by farmers in planning production and marketing, and equally needed by other market participants in arriving at optimal trading decisions. The existence and dissemination of complete and accurate marketing information is the key to achieve both operational and pricing efficiency in the marketing system. Advancement in information and communication technology (ICT) has made the world a smaller place and a larger market at one go. To fully utilize the new emerging trade opportunities for the benefit of farming community, there is a felt need to establish an ICT-based Agricultural Marketing Information Network in the country. Towards this end, Ministry of Agriculture, Government of India launched the ICT-based Central sector scheme of Agricultural Marketing Information Network (AGMARKNET) in March 2000 to link important agricultural produce markets spread all over the country and the State Agriculture Marketing Boards and Directorates. The project is being executed with the technical support of National Informatics Centre (NIC).

In order to facilitate wider market access to farm produce and better price discovery through value addition, the scheme is additionally disseminating information on market requirements in terms of quality, packing, standards, sanitary and phyto-sanitary conditions etc.

8.8.1 Objectives of the Scheme: These are the following:

1. To establish a nation-wide information network for speedy collection and dissemination of market information and data for its efficient and timely utilization.
2. To facilitate collection and dissemination of information related to better price realization by the farmers. This would cover:

- Market-related information such as market fee, market charges, costs, method of sale, payment, weighment, handling, market functionaries, development programmes, market laws, dispute settlement mechanism, composition of market committees, income and expenditure etc.
- Price-related information such as minimum, maximum and modal prices of varieties and qualities transacted, total arrivals and dispatches with destination, marketing costs and margins etc.
- Infrastructure-related information comprising facilities and services available to the farmers with regard to storage and warehousing, cold storage, direct marketing, contract farming, buy-back arrangements, grading, re-handling and repacking etc.
- Promotion-related information covering accepted standards and grades, labelling, sanitary and phyto-sanitary requirements, pledge finance, marketing credit and new opportunities available in respect of better marketing.

3. To sensitize and orient farmers to respond to new challenges in agricultural marketing by using ICT as a

vehicle of extension.

4. To improve efficiency in agricultural marketing through regular training and extension for reaching region-specific farmers in their own language.
5. To provide assistance for marketing research to generate marketing information for its dissemination to farmers and other marketing functionaries at grass-root level to create an ambience of good marketing practices in the country.

8.8.2 Proposed Activities: The Scheme will continue during the Eleventh Five Year Plan (2007-12) by enhancing its scope to cover 500 additional markets including remaining principal regulated markets, if any, farmer/consumer markets, private markets, panchayat markets, urban markets and special commodity markets. Following activities are also proposed to be undertaken while implementing the Scheme during the Eleventh Plan to fully achieve various objectives of the Scheme:

1. Information regarding export documentation, export infrastructure, transportation facilities, exporters, marketing experts, agri-business corporate, quality standards, grading/packhouse infrastructure, plant quarantine facilities, package of best marketing practices, seasonality of commodities will be provided on the portal.
2. Information on contract farming, direct marketing opportunities, value addition facilities etc. to be enriched and tie-ups between farmers/growers and sponsors/buyers will be facilitated through the portal by evolving a specific software system through outsourcing of work to an expert agency. It would be developed as an interactive query based system to educate the farmers on issues raised by them and would serve as a national clearing house for buyback and contract farming arrangements.
3. Information on warehouses along with addresses, accreditation facilities and their distance, pledge financing facilities etc. will also be provided on the portal.
4. Area specific success stories will be loaded at the portal so

that farmers get knowledge and can plan for trading of their produce.

5. GIS-based atlas will be expedited for the content enrichment and system will be put in place for regular data updating.
6. A data validation software will be developed to identify the wrong reporting and for removal of undesirable data from the central data base.
7. Electronic display boards will be provided at every networked market for displaying minimum and maximum price of important commodities, arrivals, temperature etc. These efforts would be dovetailed, as far as possible, with the action being taken by the Forward Market Commission under the Scheme of the Department of Consumer Affairs.
8. Translation of contents of portal into regional languages is necessary and this work will be undertaken through the concerned State Marketing Boards/Directorates.
9. Strategic alliances will be developed with corporate, telecom players and private users for strengthening market intelligence services.

Promotion of nationally and internationally acceptable standards of grading and standardization, packaging and labelling, storage and warehousing and sanitary and phyto-sanitary requirements and quality certification in farm sector will enable trade and processing sector to undertake large scale agricultural marketing operations in domestic as well as international markets.

8.9 Eleventh Five Year Plan (2007-12) on Agricultural Marketing

Expressing concern about the unsatisfactory state of markets for agricultural produce, the Eleventh Plan Document remarked, "The markets lack even basic infrastructure at many places. When the APMCs, were first initiated there was significant gain in market infrastructure development. However, this infrastructure is now out of date, especially given the needs of a diversified agriculture. At present only one-fourth of the markets have common drying yards, trader modules viz. shop, godown, and platform in front of shop exist in only 63 percent of the markets. Cold storage units are needed in the markets where perishable commodities are brought for sale But exist only in 9 percent of the markets at present and grading facilities exist in less than one-third of the markets. The basic facilities viz. internal roads, boundary walls, electric lights, loading and unloading facilities and weighing equipment are available in more than 80 percent of the markets. Farmers' rest houses exist in more than half of the regulated markets. Covered or open auction platforms exist in only 2/3rd of the regulated markets. It is evident from the above that there is considerable gap in the facilities available in the market yards. Also the farmers have to deal with non-transparent methods of price discovery and there is often lack of auction of graded items. Some modern markets will electronic auctioning have been introduced, but they are the exception. A major modernisation of this aspect of the infrastructure is urgently needed". [2]

8.10 Measures to Improve Agricultural Marketing

Defects in the present system of agricultural marketing can be removed by providing the following facilities to the farmers:

1. In view of the poverty of the Indian farmers, it is necessary to provide them with credit facilities at the time of harvest so that they are not forced to sell their produce at that time. Soon after the harvest, the prices of agricultural products are relatively low. Farmers should have the choice to wait for better times, i.e. better prices. This can be done by providing them with short-term credit to build their staying power.
2. If the farmers decide to postpone the sale of their produce in view of low prices at the time of harvest, they should have proper warehousing facilities. Government should provide scientific storage facilities at reasonable charges in or near the villages. This task can be entrusted to the Central

Warehousing Corporation and the State Warehousing Corporations.

3. Next in logical order are the transport facilities. Villages in India are not well connected with cities and townships through *pucca* roads or railways. If efficient transport facilities are available to farmers throughout the year, they can take their produce to markets of their choice to secure remunerative prices.
4. It is also necessary to provide adequate and latest information to the farmers regarding prices of various agricultural commodities prevailing in different markets. Although this is being done through radio and television, there is the need to extend the coverage of these facilities to all parts of the country.
5. Farmers should be provided with reasonable amenities in the *mandies*. Efforts should be made to reduce the presence of large number of middlemen in the *mandies* who erode profits of the farmers considerably. Arrangements should exist for grading and standardisation of agricultural produce. Moreover, provision should be made for following facilities in the *mandies,* viz. post office, banking, lodging and boarding for overnight stay and parking for vehicles.

Improvement in the marketing system will go a long way to ensure remunerative prices to the farmers, inducing them to produce more.

End Notes

1. Government of India, Ministry of Agriculture, Department of Agriculture and Co-operation, *National Policy for Farmers*, 2007, pp. 16-17.
2. Government of India, Planning Commission, *Eleventh Five Year Plan* (2007-12), Volume III. p. 22.

9

Agricultural Price Policy and Public Distribution System (PDS)

The objectives of a sound agricultural price policy are two-fold: (a) to ensure fair prices for the produce of the farmers, and (b) to ensure adequate and regular supply of agricultural commodities to the consumers at reasonable prices. Excessive fluctuations in agricultural prices generate harmful effects both for the producers and the consumers.

The beneficiaries of unstable prices are the middlemen and the speculators. It is for these reasons that Government undertakes buffer stocks operations, i.e. making purchases when there is glut of produce in the market and releasing stocks during period of scarcity. The price policy also seeks to evolve a balanced and integrated price structure in the perspective of the overall needs of the economy. Towards this end, the Government announces each season the minimum support prices (MSPs) for major agricultural commodities and organizes purchase operations through public, co-operative and other agencies designated by the State Governments.

9.1 Minimum Support Prices (MSPs)

An important element of the agricultural price policy of the Government of India is the announcement every year of minimum support prices for major commodities. The co-operative societies and government agencies have helped the farmers to escape the exploitative practices of the private traders.

9.1.1 Background of MSPs: The price support policy of the Government is directed at providing insurance to agricultural producers against any sharp fall in farm prices. The minimum guaranteed prices are fixed to set a floor below which market prices cannot fall. Till the mid-1970s, Government announced two types of administered prices: (a) minimum support prices (MSPa), and (b) procurement prices. MSPs served as the floor prices and were fixed by the Government in the nature of a long-term guarantee for investment decisions of producers, with the assurance that prices of their commodities would not be allowed to fall below the level fixed by the Government, even in the case of a bumper crop.

Procurement prices were the prices of kharif and rabi cereals at which the grain was to be domestically procured by public agencies like the Food Corporation of India (FCI) for release through PDS. It was announced soon after harvest began. Normally, procurement price was lower than the open market price and higher than the MSP. This policy of two official prices being announced continued with some variation up to 1973-74, in the case of paddy. In the case of wheat it was discontinued in 1969 and then revived in 1974-75 for one year only. Since there were too many demands for stepping up the MSP, the present system was evolved in 1975 in which only one set of prices is announced for paddy (and other kharif crops) and wheat being procured for buffer stock operations.

9.1.2 Methodology for Cost Calculation: The minimum support prices for major agricultural products are announced each year after taking into account the recommendations of the Commission for Agricultural Costs and Prices (CACP). The CACP, while recommending prices takes into account all important factors including cost of production, changes in input prices, input/output price parity, trends in market prices, inter-crop parity, demand and supply situation, parity between prices paid and prices received by farmers etc. Among these multiple factors that go into the formulation of support price policy, the cost of production is the most significant. Thus, for making the support price policy functionally meaningful, the minimum guaranteed prices ought to cover at least the reasonable cost of production in a normal agricultural season obtained from efficient farming.

The CACP analyses the cost of production data for various states in respect of various commodities in consultation with the states. After a meeting of the State Chief Ministers, the MPS/procurement prices are declared. With costs of production for the same crops varying between regions and also across farms within the same region and for different producers, the level of costs that could be accepted as a norm poses enormous difficulties.

In fixing the support prices, CACP relies on the cost concept which covers all items of expenses of cultivation including in that the imputed value of inputs owned by farmers such as rental value of owned land and interest on fixed capital. Some of the important cost concepts used by CACP are the C2 and C3 costs.

C2 cost includes all actual expenses in cash and kind incurred in production by actual owner plus rent paid for leased land plus imputed value of family labour plus interest on value of owned capital assets (excluding land) plus rental value of owned land (net of land revenue).

C3 cost means cost C2 + 10 percent of cost C2 to account for managerial remuneration to the farmer.

Costs of production are calculated both on per quintal and per hectare basis. Presently, the following crops are covered under the mechanism of MSPs:

- **Cereals:** paddy, wheat, jowar, bajra, maize, *ragi* and barley.
- **Pulses:** moong, *urad, arhar*, gram, lentil and peas.
- **Oilseeds:** groundnut, rapeseed and mustard, niger seed, soybean, sunflower, sesamum and safflower.
- **Fibre Crops:** cotton and jute.
- **Others:** sugarcane, VFC tobacco, onion, potato and coconut.

Trends in the MSP of wheat and paddy in recent years are given in Table 9.1.

Table 9.1: Minimum Support/Procurement Prices of Wheat and Paddy in Recent Years (₹/quintal)

Crop Year	Wheat	Paddy (common)
1997-98	510	415
1998-99	550	440
1999-00	580	490
2000-01	610	510
2001-02	620	530
2002-03	620	530
2003-04	630	550
2004-05	640	560
2005-06	650	570
2006-07	750	580
2008-09	1,080	900
2010-11	1,120	1,000
2011-12	1,285	1,080
2012-13	1,350	1,250

Source: Government of India, *Economic Survey* (various years).

Realising the importance of inter-sectoral terms of trade [1], the Government of India modified the terms of reference for CACP. Consequently, CACP has been regularly taking into account the terms of trade ever since 1980 while recommending support/procurement prices for agricultural commodities.

In the meantime, Government of India constituted a Task Force in March 1993 (Chairman: A.S. Kahlon) to suggest methodology for constructing an index of terms of trade between agricultural and non-agricultural sectors. The Government now computes the terms of trade between the two sectors on the basis of the methodology recommended by the Task Force.

9.1.3 Economic Cost of Foodgrains to Food Corporation of India (FCI): The economic cost of foodgrains to FCI is of strategic importance, as it influences not only the food subsidy bill but also the country's competitiveness in international markets for foodgrains. The FCI is reimbursed the difference between the economic cost of foodgrains and the issue price. The economic cost of foodgrains to FCI has been on the rise over the years. The increase in the MSPs of rice and wheat, high State-level levies, and the rising trend in distribution costs have contributed to the increase in the economic costs of foodgrains over the years.

The major procurement States—Punjab, Haryana and Andhra Pradesh—have been imposing State taxes and levies of over 10 percent ad valorem on the procurement of foodgrains, thereby inflating the economic cost.

9.2 Food Subsidy

Producers and consumers and within this group the vulnerable sections of the society are the major beneficiaries of food subsidy. The subsidy incurred on the supply of foodgrains through the PDS at below FCI's economic cost constitutes the consumer subsidy while the producer subsidy is the direct offshoot of the price support based procurement operations of the Government. The producer subsidy together with the cost of maintaining the buffer stock accounts for the cost of buffer stock operations. The consumer subsidy together with the buffer carrying cost constitutes the food subsidy.

The food subsidy bill has increased from year to year in recent times (Table 9.2). Though pruning of the existing subsidy level is imperative and could be done by reducing operational inefficiency, the interests of the poor also have to be safeguarded. The surplus stocks of foodgrains with the Government provide a vital resource for providing income support to the poor and the vulnerable. Better targeting of subsidies is now beginning to be visible. However, it has been found that PDS has failed in large parts of the country, and that it needs to be restructured to be an effective tool of food security.

MSPs lay the floor for the market price of foodgrains, especially the two dominant foodgrains: rice and wheat. With sharp increases in MSP every year despite surpluses having replaced shortages, the MSPs have become the maximum selling price instead of being the floor price. This coupled with the system of open-ended procurement has made FCI the buyer of the first resort resulting in huge accumulation of surplus public stocks of foodgrains, leading to much higher commitments for Government subsidy. FCI has thus become the main buyer, stockist and seller in the domestic market. It is also the main exporter.

Table 9.2: Growth of Food Subsidies in India in Recent Years

(₹ crore)

Year	Food Subsidy
2001-02	17,494
2002-03	24,176
2003-04	25,160
2004-05	25,746
2005-06	23,071
2006-07	23,827
2007-08	31,259
2008-09	43,668
2009-10	58,242
2010-11	62,929

Source: Government of India, *Economic Survey,* 2011-12, p. 198, Table 8.14.

High statutory levies (including mandi charges, cesses and fees to commission agents) on grain purchase, not only discourage private trade but also increase FCI's cost, thus putting a pressure on the food subsidy bill. The levies imposed by the State Governments (ad valorem) differ from State to State and are highest in case of Punjab, Haryana and Andhra Pradesh.

The High Level Committee on Long Term Grain Policy recommended that Government may, for open-ended procurement, in future announce a gross price, inclusive of MSP and a uniform 4 percent allowance for State taxes as the price that its agencies would be allowed to pay. It would be better for the centre and states to agree on a ceiling on statutory levies, and announce MSPs which farmers could actually expect to receive net of all compulsory levies.

In order to achieve the objective of targeting subsidies sharply to the poor and the truly needy, the Ministry of Finance with the assistance of the National Institute of Public Finance and Policy (NIPFP) prepared a report on Central Government Subsidies in India. The report examined major subsidies including food and fertilisers and recommended policies for reforms in subsidies. As regards food subsidies, the report suggested that the minimum support prices should be kept at the C2 level recommended by the CACP. To contain operational costs, reimbursement of expenses of the FCI should be based on normative unit costs and actual quantities involved. With respect to the PDS, it is suggested that the system of dual prices, which encourages leakages, may be replaced by a uniform price policy along with a system of food coupons for the BPL families.

9.3 Public Distribution System (PDS)

Food security is one of the major components of social security. There is enough food available in India. What is required is a well-organised public distribution system. Efforts have been made to streamline the PDS through the introduction of the Targeted Public Distribution System (TPDS) in June 1997. This system follows a two-tier subsidised pricing structure for families below poverty line (BPL) and for those above poverty line (APL). BPL population receives rice and wheat at a much lower price (hence highly subsidised) whereas APL population is supplied at a price which is much higher and closer to the economic cost. The identification of the poor under the scheme is done by the States.

PDS is the cornerstone of Government's price policy and food security system in India. It ensures availability of certain essential commodities (sugar, kerosene, rice and wheat) at affordable prices, especially for the poor. Through its agency the Food Corporation of India (FCI), the Government procures and stocks foodgrains, which are released every month for distribution through the PDS network across the country. These commodities are distributed to the public through a network of fair price shops (FPS). In addition to this, the system of procurement is also used by the Government to provide minimum support prices to the farmers in order to stabilise agricultural output and income.

The FCI issues foodgrains to the State Governments at a uniform central issue price (CIP) which is considerably lower than the economic cost incurred by the Central Government by way of procurement, storage, transport and distribution. The difference between the economic cost and the CIP is called the consumer subsidy. Since the FCI maintains a large buffer stock of foodgrains, it entails a substantial carrying cost. The consumer subsidy and the carrying cost together add up to the total food subsidy which is borne by the Central Government. It is an important item of the non-Plan revenue expenditure of the Government as shown in its annual budget.

9.3.1 Targeted Public Distribution System (TPDS): A well-targeted and properly functioning PDS is an important constituent of the strategy for poverty alleviation. PDS is operated under the joint responsibility of the Central and State Governments. The Central Government takes the responsibility for procurement, storage, transportation and bulk allocation of foodgrains, at subsidized prices. The responsibility of distribution to consumers including target groups through a network of fair price shops rests with the State Governments.

TPDS was introduced in 1997 in order to achieve better targeting of food subsidy. Under the TPDS, a dual price mechanism for above the poverty line (APL) and below the poverty line (BPL) consumers prevails. The full economic cost of foodgrains is recovered from the APL consumers while foodgrains are sold at half the economic cost to BPL consumers.

Criticising the present system of differential PDS pricing, Mid-term Appraisal of Tenth Five Year Plan (June 2005), observed, "The present system of differential PDS pricing, with very low prices for BPL consumers, is a highly inefficient way of serving the equity objective. There are heavy leakages of as much as 55 percent according to a recent Planning Commission study. The system also distorts incentives for grain producers in non-surplus areas where FCI procurement is poor or non-existent, because it depresses grain prices below the MSP. With the Food for Work Programme in place and the expansion of Mid-Day Meals and the universalisation of Integrated Child Development Services (ICDS), there is a strong case for moving to uniform PDS pricing. In other words, the PDS, should not be viewed as a poverty reducing instrument as much as an instrument for protecting the common man (including the poor) by stabilising issue prices at a level which may imply only a limited subsidy but which insulates the consumer from sudden increases in prices due to scarcity. The procurement side of the operation should continue to aim at stabilising MSP reasonably above costs of production. Procurement support should also be extended to cover the entire country.

PDS pricing is a sensitive issue, but the proposed change is a logical consequence of the adoption of other schemes aimed at poverty alleviation. It needs to be implemented in parallel with the expansion of other social safety net schemes. The resources saved by moving towards a unified issue price should be directed to expand other poverty reducing programmes, including especially the FFW.

The urban poor are not covered by the Food for work Programme and a case can be made that they need continued subsidy benefits through the PDS. This could be attempted through a system of smart cards. A smart card may be charged with the entitlement of the person who can buy ration commodities from any trader who is linked to the smart card system. The price difference can be automatically transferred to the traders account when the holder makes a purchase." [2]

9.4 High Level Committee on Long-term Grain Policy

The Government had constituted a High Level Committee on November 16, 2000 for formulating a long-term grain policy for the country. The Committee submitted its final report on July 31, 2002. Some of the recommendations made by the Committee for long-term grain management are listed below:

1. Quality norms should be strictly adhered to while procuring foodgrains for PDS distribution.
2. Payments as statutory levies to State Governments by FCI are essentially transfers from the Centre to the States. These should be taken care of separately between the Centre and the States without involving the FCI.
3. MSP for paddy should be fixed only for a single grade.
4. APL price should be reduced to 80 percent of the economic cost and BPL price to 50 percent of the economic cost excluding statutory levies. This would also help improve the viability of the fair price shops in the distribution network.
5. Once the current high stocks are reduced, the resultant savings could be used for employment schemes, for which there is a strong felt need and which could be used to develop rural infrastructure.
6. Existing Antyodaya scheme of food support should be expanded to become a food security system for the entire destitute population.
7. A system of universal PDS should be introduced with uniform CIP, one each for rice and wheat respectively, for all consumers in all parts of the country.
8. Central Government should announce its MSP policy before the sowing season on recommendations of the Commission for Agricultural Costs and Prices (CACP).
9. CACP should be made an empowered statutory body.
10. In recommending MSPs which should apply only to fair

average quality grain, the CACP should go strictly on the basis of C2 cost of production (i.e. all costs including imputed costs of family labour, owned capital and rental on land) in more efficient regions.

11. While the Centre has to continue to take the primary responsibility for procurement, as production is dispersed procurement should also become more dispersed and this process can definitely save costs of transportation and meet consumer needs more adequately.
12. All compulsory levy orders on rice millers under the Essential Commodities Act (ECA) should be removed with immediate effect.
13. A different problem likely to arise as a result of lower MSPs is that there will be a probability for market prices to exceed MSP and, therefore, quantities offered for sale at MSP may fall short of PDS and buffer stocks requirements. In situations where market conditions are such that MSP purchases fall short of PDS requirements, Government would need to make purchases on the basis of best terms. This may include imports, open market purchases from secondary markets or through open tender purchases or purchases from farmers at market-determined prices above MSP.
14. Crop diversification is very important at the current stage of India's agricultural development, given the changing dietary patterns. There is need for special packages for diversification.
15. There should be an automatic and transparent policy of variable tariffs on both agricultural imports and exports linked to the deviation of spot international prices from their long-run trends. This is required for stabilisation of prices in an open economy.
16. Barriers to private trade, economic as well as legal, should be eased.
17. FCI has performed its role in its core functions reasonably well and should continue to do so keeping in mind that

there has to be a work culture of total quality management.

18. It is desirable that that the FCI's role be confined to procurement of the major cereals for the PDS and that price support operations in coarse cereals be handled by State agencies.

9.5 Task Force on IT Strategy for PDS

This Task Force (Chairman: Nandan Nilekani) was constituted by the Planning Commission to recommend an IT strategy for PDS reform and suggest a solution for direct transfer of subsidies on kerosene, LPG, and fertilizer to the intended beneficiaries. The terms of reference of the Task Force were as follows:

1. To identify and suggest required changes in the existing systems, processes and procedures.
2. To suggest IT frameworks and supply chain management.
3. To recommend institutional mechanisms to implement IT strategy for the PDS.
4. To examine and suggest an implementable solution for direct transfer of subsidies on food and kerosene to intended beneficiaries with the use of Aadhaar (Unique Identification Numbers), Aadhaar-enabled transactions, and Aadhaar authentication infrastructure.

The Task Force submitted its report in October 2011 and made the following main recommendations:

1. Set up a strong, robust IT infrastructure backbone to reform the functioning of PDS which would be an incentive-based system for all stakeholders.
2. End-to-end computerization of PDS across the country and provision of a token-agnostic technology solution that can accept physical coupons, smartcards, electronic coupons, and facilitate direct cash transfers.
3. PDS Network (PDSN), as the National Information Utility (NIU) to be the common software platform for all States, to implement and operate the IT infrastructure for PDS. PDSN as the technology back office would manage all IT

operations related to PDS with focus on supply chain management to address leakages, real time fraud analytics, entitlement portability and transparent grievance redressal channel.

4. Aadhaar (UIN) to be used in PDS to simplify ration card registration, cleaning up the beneficiary database; State Governments can use Aadhaar Payments Bridge and Aadhaar-enabled payment systems to channel subsidy funds for approved commodities to Aadhaar-enabled bank accounts.
5. Provision of maximum choice to the beneficiaries in terms of location, mix of commodities, convenient quantities and in any number of instalments; and choice to purchase commodities or receive a direct transfer of subsidy.
6. Organizational structure to operationalise the PDS to consist of a Governing Board appointed by the shareholders of PDSN which includes Government of India and other stakeholders with the Chairman of the Board appointed by Government of India. The CEO of PDSN would be selected through an open selection process by the Board.
7. Set up a core subsidy management system (CSMS) for direct transfer of subsidies on kerosene, LPG, and fertilizer through Aadhar-enabled bank account (AEBA) to facilitate robust identification of the beneficiary. The CSMS would support all forms of direct transfers of subsidies such as non-cash transfers, conditional cash transfers, direct cash transfers etc. CSMS would be responsive to the needs of beneficiaries, provide increased transparency, grievance redressal and real time transfer of funds.
8. Fertilizers movement and sale at market price, with reimbursement of subsidy directly to the beneficiary, to reduce the incentive for pilferage due to two prices of the same commodity.

To sum up, Government's price policy for agricultural

produce seeks to ensure remunerative prices to growers for their produce with a view to encouraging higher investment and production and safeguarding the interests of consumers by making available food supplies at reasonable prices. The price policy also seeks to evolve a balanced and integrated price structure in keeping with the overall needs of the economy.

To achieve this end, the government announces minimum support prices (MSPs) for major agricultural commodities each season and organizes purchase operations through the Food Corporation of India, and cooperative and other agencies designated by state governments. The government decides on the MSPs for various agricultural commodities taking into account the recommendations of the Commission for Agricultural Costs and Prices (CACP), the views of State Governments and Central Ministries as well as such other relevant factors which are considered important for fixation of support prices.

The Government decides on the support price for various agricultural commodities taking into account the recommendations of the CACP, the views of State Governments and Central Ministries as well as such other relevant factors which, in the opinion of the Government, are important for fixation of support prices.

PDS is recognised as a permanent feature of the strategy to control prices, reduce fluctuations and achieve an equitable distribution of essential goods. An efficient public distribution system requires a nexus between production, procurement, transportation, storage, and distribution of the selected commodities.

The working of the PDS is periodically reviewed in consultation with the State Governments and corrective measures are taken from time to time to improve the supply of various essential commodities to the consumers.

End Notes

1. Terms of trade between the agricultural and non-agricultural sectors is a subject of controversy among agricultural

economists in India. Terms of trade are defined as the ratio of agricultural prices to non-agricultural prices. There are two schools of thought. According to one, terms of trade have moved in favour of the agricultural sector with the result that the development of the industrial sector has slowed down. Hence, it is contended that agricultural prices should be lowered to give a boost to industries.

Contrarily, many hold the view that terms of trade have moved against the farm sector and therefore higher agricultural prices are needed to induce the farmers to produce more. The debate is inconclusive because the results of various studies are conflicting due to different methodologies and assumptions adopted by the researchers.

2. Government of India, Planning Commission, *Mid-term Appraisal of Tenth Five Year Plan*, June 2005, pp. 6-7.

Appendix

Appendix

Agrarian Structure of Odisha in Retrospect and Prospect

Odisha is primarily an agrarian economy. Agriculture is the State's dominant sector with contribution of nearly 23.40 percent to net state domestic product (including animal husbandry) during 2005-06 at 1993-94 prices. The agriculture alone provides direct and indirect employment to around 65 percent of the total workforce of the state (2001 Census). Nevertheless, the sector is characterized by low productivity and is over crowded with rising dependant population. Therefore, agricultural growth, agricultural activities and land holding pattern, hold key to the economic development of the State by way of creating employment, generating income, providing raw materials to the industrial sector and last but not the least, ensuring self-reliance in food production and food security to the deprived sections. But, the structure of distribution of land ownership and its operational holdings at present may have critical impact on agricultural production, productivity, food security and livelihood of the rural population.

One may not have a clear cut insight into the present day agrarian problems and the performance of agricultural sector in the State unless one is well versed with the metamorphosis of the land system and the agrarian structure of the State over time. Agrarian structure implies the conditions and relations of land and man in ever changing time and space. [1] The land structure of Odisha has developed over a long evolutionary process. It is aptly remarked "comprehension of present day agrarian problems would be incomprehensible without analyzing their historical roots. Because history is closely and in different ways connected with the battle for ownership and utilization of agricultural land. This seems natural in a country like ours and so also, in a poverty-stricken state like Odisha, where the overwhelming majority of population live on land and the whole internal and external economy is still largely dependent on the production of this sector". [2]

During the Hindu rule, for the sake of revenue administration, the whole kingdom was divided into certain broad divisions called *mandals* and each mandal was sub-divided into *vishyas* which more or less correspond to modern districts. The vishyas are also sub-divided in to smaller units known as Bhoga, Bhakti, Khanda, Panchali and the smallest unit was *grama* or village. But during the period of Gangas and Gajapaties, the designations of revenue divisions were changed from Mandal to Dandapat, Vishya to Bisa or Bisi. During this Hindu rule, the king was not the absolute owner of the soil. The right of perpetual occupancy was conferred on the cultivators. The proprietary intermediate class of succeeding period did not exist.

During the Mughal period there were some forces at work, which were capable of transforming the agrarian structure full of peasant proprietors in the land system and also full of tenants. With the passage of time, Odishan agricultural society was steadily transformed and developed over a period of time apparently or inapparently, lawfully or unlawfully into a kind of landlord-tenant relationship during that rule.

However, British conquest was a decisive turning point in the evolution of Odishan land tenure system as it was accompanied by a revolutionary action of conferring legal recognition to various types of landed proprietors. This paved the way for the complete destruction of traditional rights of peasants vis-à-vis the creation of a full-fledged feudalistic land system. Further, this laid the foundation of an inequitable social set-up. However, the agrarian structure and the land holding system of the State has undergone transformation through the following successive generations.

Ancient Land System during Hindu Rule

The Hindu system of land ownership and land

management had prevailed in Odisha prior to the advent of Afghan and Mughal rule in the State. In the year 1568 A.D., the Afghans conquered Odisha but they have no opportunity to establish their rules. Then came the Mughals. Odisha became a part of the Mughal Empire with the conquest of Mughal General, Raja Todar Mall in 1578. During the rule of the Hindu Rajas of Odisha prior to 1568, no intermediate proprietary right of any kind was allowed to grow between the king and the tillers of the soil. The right of permanent occupancy was conferred on the cultivators. The usual custom was that the person who reclaimed and brought the virgin land under the plough became its rightful owner and enjoyed the privilege of undisturbed and perpetual possession over that land with a right to inherit. Then, the State's right to raise revenue came up.

The Rajas had the right to collect revenue in the form of a share of the produce of that cultivable land from the cultivator. The King honoured the perpetual ownership right over that land of the cultivator as long as he (cultivator) paid the revenue to the State. Therefore, in ancient Odisha, it appeared in practice that the right of individual and private ownership over land was vested in the peasants vis-à-vis the kings' unquestionable right to raise revenue. [3]

Some scholars opine that the individual property right over land was originally absent. It developed over a period of time in an evolutionary process. The historical evidences from ancient literature, archaeological materials suggest that in ancient agrarian economy of Odisha, land was originally held under the common ownership of a village community and there was no individual ownership right over land. These villages were self-sustained and the surplus produce was shared jointly by all the members of the community. But, with the passage of time, the community ownership of land got completely destroyed and it paved the way for appearance of peasant proprietorship and peasant farming at the beginning of the 'Ganga Dynasty' in the twelfth century.

During this period, half of the land of the Ganga Empire was distributed as revenue free land among the border army chiefs or frontier keepers such as Khandaits and Bhunias for their military services to the State and among Brahmins for their worship services to deities. In this connection, A.P. Sah's thesis reveals that assignment of such revenue free land to the above mentioned communities were granted only for certain services rendered by them to the State and there was no general sign of growth of any landed intermediary class in Odisha during that period. [4] Raja Anangabhima Dev had created sixteenth Sawanta Rajas who were posted all around and along the frontiers especially along the eastern and western frontiers of Utkal, the then State of Odisha.

Therefore, the land of the State at that time was divided into two principal divisions, viz. military and civil. The military land was under the possession of the military chiefs and the vast army of peasants-cum-soldiers, who cultivated the land at the time of peace and used to take up arms against the invaders during war.

Military land was confined to the hill states protected by forts where the military chiefs resided. As these lands were assigned to provide military service, they were revenue free except under extraordinary circumstances.

On the other hand, the most fertile and the vast plain of rice land along the coastal belt situated between the western and eastern frontier was known as the civil land or the crown land. This portion of the State was directly managed by the king with the help of revenue officials in order to get maximum possible land revenue. [5] This necessitated the continuance of the prevailing land revenue administration through the Hindu revenue officials. [6] But, these revenue officials were never given the proprietorship of land. The Hindu rulers did not allow the growth of any intermediate landed proprietor above the farmers because it would harm the interest of the farmers. The Hindu Rajas provided a protective hand to the peasant community by keeping the revenue as well as the land administration under their direct control and supervision.

In course of time, the hereditary revenue officers in the agrarian system were said to have developed into a class of land owners with intermediary interest. Sometimes they declared themselves as *zamindars* or practical landlords and their position became hereditary. Thus, a new intermediary interest was said to have developed during the latter part of Hindu rule in Odisha while a sizeable number of landless labourers in the productive process got a share of the produce.

Agrarian System during Mughal Rule

The second phase of socio-economic transition of agrarian structure in Odisha commenced in 1584 when Mughal General, Raja Todar Mall completed the land settlement in Odisha. As the administrator of the State of Odisha, he conducted a detailed survey and settlement in the year 1580. This settlement included the three divisions of Sarkars, viz. Cuttack, Bhadrak and Jaleswar, which then constituted the Province. Although Mughal rule in Odisha was a military occupation and land tenures and cultivation were by this fact necessarily rendered insecure, the conqueror cannot be accused of having neglected the civil administration.

The revenue system was maintained almost intact and neither officials nor peasants were subjected to plunder or extort. For the purpose of settlement, land was classified into four classes according to their capability of annual cultivation. After measurement, assessment was made on the basis of area, quality of land and average of previous 10 years produce. Raja Todar Mall for the most part, left untouched the border chieftains from settlement of revenue. Khurda together with the States of Lambai, Chaubiskhand, Rahang and Sarai was assigned to Raja Rama Chandra Dev and to the Temple of Lord Jagannath. The Raja of Khurda received the rank of Commander of 3500 and under his control were placed 31 Zamindars with 129 Killahs.

Under the Mughal rule, the old revenue division of the

province into military land and civil land (crown land) was allowed to continue. However, the military land was henceforth called 'Gadjat' or 'Killajat' or 'Rajwara' and it remained under the hill chiefs who tendered submission and agreed to pay an annual revenue either in cash or kind. The remaining area or the civil land was brought under the management and direct administration of the Mughal kings in order to get maximum possible revenue and was called Mughalbandi. It was a vast plain of rice land along with the coastal belt of Odisha. A small portion of the land of the Mughalbandi was assigned as Jagir to high military and civil personnel. The revenue of the jagir land was not paid to public exchequer, but was appropriated by the Jagirdars for their service to the State. The revenue from the major part of civil land under direct control of Mughal kings called Khalsa/Khas land was paid to the state exchequer.

It appears that the changes in the land tenure and land revenue system of Odisha consequent upon the subjection to the Mughals were very significant. The seed of feudalism was sown in the Odishan land system by the Mughals, though the feudalistic structure was not immediately developed in a full-fledged form till the British conquest of Odisha. After the Mughal conquest, the civil land known as Mughalbandi was taken away from the Raja. But, with the apprehension of rebellion from the Rajas and Royal Households, these royal families were allowed to hold a sizeable extensive area of land in *zamindari* tenure on condition of paying a fixed sum of land revenue.

This shows that the Mughals, by acknowledging a class of zamindars, laid the foundation for the growth of feudalism and a class of landed intermediary. In the latter part of the Mughal rule, with the progressive downfall of Muslim power, these royal families became so powerful that they called themselves as zamindars and imposed their legal sanction of the proprietorship over the land. Thus, the Mughal rule brought a turning point in the land tenure system of Odisha and the system continued even after the commencement of Mahratta rule in 1751.

Land Structure during Mahratta Period

Odisha had experienced fifty years of Mahratta Rule. The Mahrattas appeared in Odisha in 1742 and State was finally held under their possession in 1751. Allivardi Khan practically handed over Odisha to the hands of Mahrattas by the Treaty of 1751 A.D. The river Subarnarekha formed boundary between Bengal and Odisha whose southern frontiers extended to Malud. The Mahrattas did not make any substantial change in the revenue system and land system of Odisha existing then. They divided the Mughalbandi into four chakalas or divisions namely Cuttack, Bhadrak, Soro and Balasore and about 150 paraganas.

Mahrattas followed a system of land revenue collection under the management of thirty-two salaried revenue Officers called 'amils'. An amil was responsible for the revenue collection of each chakla, and he was assisted by a sadar kanungo under whom was a gomasta also known as vilayati kanungo, who made the mofasil (revenue) collections. About one-eighth of the total revenue paying area was so held by makadams though it had previously been the custom to make a yearly detailed computation of rentals on which the makadam was allowed a percentage for collection expenses. Towards the close of the century, the 'amils' found it convenient to take engagements from them for a lump sum.

It was Raja Ram Pandit, the enlightened Mahratta Subadar who first started to dispense with the talukdars, the collecting agents of Mughals, in 1773. These talukdars were replaced by the vilayati kanungos for making collection of revenue directly from the roytas and paying them over sadar kanungos to the 'amils'. The sadar kanungo who generally stood security for the payment of revenue by the talukdars, was allowed in case of default to take over the taluk on payment of arrears by him. At the beginning of the British conquest, both sadar and vilayati kanungos were found in possession of a large number of estates. They settled mostly with village-level and land holding interest like Kanungos and Choudhuries.

The Marathas dispossessed a number of superior tenure holders and collected directly from the heads of the village guilds. All their efforts were directed towards extracting as much revenue from the conquered States. Peasants and officials were alike subjected to every exaction and exploitation by the Mahrattas. Their rule was detrimental to the welfare and the prosperity of the state.

Mr. Maddox aptly remarked, "cultivation was attended with no security, rights were everywhere neglected and denied. The peasant was accustomed to regard a demand for rent not as a legitimate tax but as an exorbitant extortion and the policy of his rulers taught him a contempt for right and a disregard for duty. To this period, is to be traced a moral and social degeneration from which, I believe, the people have never entirely recovered". [7] During the closing years of Mahratta's administration, land, the chief source of income and livelihood of bulk of population in Odisha had been noticeably neglected. So, during Mahratta rule, no such significant socio-economic transition of agrarian structure took place in Odisha.

Land Structure during British Period

The third phase of socio-economic transition of agrarian structure in Odisha started with the British Rule. The British administration in Odisha, in fact, started in 1803 when the East India Company's troops took only two months to occupy Odisha after breaking down the feeble Maratha resistance. The English expedition for the conquest started from South from Ganjam on 8th September, 1803 and from North from Jaleswar on 23rd September, 1803. Puri fell to the British on 28th September, and Barabati Fort on 10th October in the year 1803. The British Administration in Odisha brought about a complete transformation of Odishan agriculture and its land tenure system.

In June 1804, for the sake of revenue administration the province of Odisha was divided into two divisions: Northern and Southern with river Mahanadi as the boundary between them, each under a Collector. Robert Ker and Charies Greme were appointed as the Judge, Magistrate and Collector of the Northern Division and Southern Division respectively. J. Hunter was sent to Puri as acting Collector of Lord Jagannath. By Regulation XIII of 1805, the two divisions were amalgamated and was placed under one Collector, with headquarters at Puri. Tehsildars were stationed at Balasore, Jajpur and Khurda and the fourth held charge of Khas Mahals. In the year 1817, the headquarters was shifted from Puri to Cuttack under the petition of Zamidars.

By Government order on 23rd October 1928, the province was divided into three districts namely Balasore, Cuttack and Jagannath (later known as Puri). Messers R. Rickets, R. Hunter and W. Wilkinson were appointed as first Magistrate and Collector of Balasore, Cuttack and Puri respectively. The districts of Ganjam and Koraput were formed a part of the newly created Odisha Province on 1st April 1936 on being separated from Madras Presidency and the district Sambalpur was also created after separated from Bihar.

Thus, during British period various parts of Odisha were under different political administrations of neighbouring Provinces and the eastern States of the British India. Therefore, land reform measures during the British period were not uniform, but rather a combination of heterogeneous measures, influenced and administered by the Land Reform Acts and administrative machineries of different Provinces. Therefore, during British period the land revenue system in Odisha had three important features: first, Bengal land revenue system (zamindari system) prevailed in Cuttack, Puri and Balasore districts; second, Madras land revenue system (Raiyatwari system) was in vogue in Ganjam and Koraput districts and third, the central province land revenue system (Mahalwari system) prevailed in Sambalpur district.

Before giving a brief account of the land structure, the land tenure system and land settlements in Odisha during British Period, we must know the basic motive and objective of land policy introduced in India by the British. The British rule in India can be divided into two periods: (i) the rule of the East India Company ranging from 1757 to 1858, and (ii) the rule of the British Government in India from 1858 to 1947. During those periods, the two outstanding developments took place in traditional agrarian set up of India.

First, during the rule of the East India Company, there was a growth of a new land tenure system through changes in property rights.

Second, during the rule of the British Government in India there developed a market economy through commercialization of agriculture by producing crops for sale rather than for family consumption. The Britishers after consolidating political power in India brought these changes in the traditional agrarian structure for the maximization of revenue and rent for the State and for an effective management of the economy. Directors of the East India Company were keen on securing the largest possible revenue. This policy was marked by excessive exactions from peasants not realizing that in the process the British were killing the goose that laid the golden egg. But land revenue was principal source of finance for the company administration in India. [8] The new land system and commercialization of Indian agriculture produced deep economic consequences on the Indian economy. These consequences rather retarded the process of industrialization in India.

India's invasion by the British brought about, in the course of time, a complete transformation in the country's land tenure system. The East India Company experienced difficulty in its trading because the sale of British goods in India was insignificant. On the other hand, the exportation of gold and silver from England to pay for Indian goods was soon prohibited. The company found a solution by securing money from India to pay for Indian goods. It collected taxes for the Indian rulers which, in the beginning, brought revenues of only 10 percent of the levied taxes, but, since the control over the amount of levied taxes became lax at the end of the Mughal period, its revenues increased. In addition, they were assigned areas as *jagir*. The decisive breakthrough came when, in 1765, the office of *dewani* for Bengal, Odisha, and Bihar, namely the financial sovereignty for these areas, was assigned to the Company with the concession for levying taxes in exchange for a global sum of ₹ 2.6 million per annum.

After a brief time of experimentation, in 1793, Cornwallis' Permanent Settlement brought a final regulation of the procedure for levying taxes, which led to decisive changes in land tenure. The British did as if all the land belonged to the state and was thus at their disposal. They registered the local tax collectors, who were called zamindars, as owners of the land in their district. These zamindars had to collect and deliver the taxes—the amount was fixed at the beginning and remained the same permanently.

To give them an incentive, they were free to decide how much to demand from the cultivators. On the other hand, the fixed lump sum tax was an incentive to put more land under cultivation and, thus, have more taxpayers in one region. Being guided by the commercial motive, the colonial government resorted to all sorts of unfair means to maximize revenue which was detrimental to agricultural development. Peasants were left to the mercies of zamindars and all sorts of sub-proprietary class for exploitation. The intermediary class also supported such policies of the government as they were the creation of Administrator, Lord Cornwallis since the introduction of Permanent Settlement in 1793. The new land system and the commercial agriculture brought untold miseries and exploitation of the Indian peasantry and the country was consequently plagued by frequent famines. The spread of irrigation, creation of revenue settlement, expansion of education, and the growth of railways etc. were all initiated with one supreme goal, i.e. to accelerate the process of economic drain in India. [9]

During British rule, land was considered as the key resource, the status symbol and a major source of revenue for collection of rent. Imposition of tax and appropriation of larger land revenue for the state formed the basic task of the British-Indian administration. Keeping this objective at the backdrop, the British administrators brought changes in property rights of different tenure holders and introduced reforms in land revenue structure. All agricultural land policies were designed with the objective to realize maximum revenue for the State. Keeping the agrarian structure apparently much the same as before, they only changed the property rights of tenure holders and conferred legal sanctions to property rights of different intermediary and landed aristocratic groups with a view to extract maximum land revenue from cultivators through native landed aristocratic intermediary class.

Accordingly "a bourgeois super structure was imposed on feudal production relations. [10] The right to the land conferred on the zamindars was alienable, rentable, and heritable. This meant the introduction of a complete novelty, in India. The privilege of utilizing land had become a saleable good. Those who had been cultivators until then, obtained the status of 'occupancy tenants'.

These occupancy rights were heritable and transferable and were not tampered with as long as the holders paid their taxes. In contrast to these, the tenants who cultivated land owned by the tax collectors were 'tenants at will', i.e. they could be evicted.

The peasant class was extremely hit by the British rule whose primary concern was to secure the highest possible revenue income from land. A number of Western and Indian scholars have brought out striking studies on agrarian problems emerging from diverse land system, operational of land laws etc. during British period with nationalistic, pragmatic and Marxian interpretations depicting imperial impact on the rural economy, zamindar-peasant relations, exploitation of peasantry by revenue collection, growth of landless peasantry, rural poverty and indebtedness, recurrent famines, commercialization of agriculture, emergence of a very small section of affluent land holders and the effect of these on the colonial agrarian structure of India.

The continuance of the same system of zamindari is also evident in Odisha. Instances are galore of the peasants being exploited and oppressed by the zamindars and other intermediary class.

In Odisha, the British administration introduced a series of temporary settlement unlike Bengal's permanent settlement. This is because in the early years of Company's rule, its administrators were in the illusion that peasants of Odisha were hiding their real yield of land. So, through short-term settlement, the company tried to extract such surplus yield, if any, and maximize states revenues. But such illusion proved false as the paying capacity of peasants was very low due to frequent failure of crops caused by cyclone, flood, drought, famine and other natural calamities.

Thus, their inability to pay rent on time often made some of the native zamindars and sub-proprietors defaulters and in consequence of their failure to pay their rent to the State, they lost their zamindari estates due to the enforcement of draconian 'sun-set laws' or 'sales laws' of auction. The temporary zamindari settlement proved detrimental to agricultural development. It was felt and pointed out by the zamindars of Odisha that the long-term settlements were necessary to bring about improvement in the condition of Raiyats. So, the zamindars pressed for permanent settlements before the British Government. But the British Government rejected the entire theory of permanent settlement. Frequent short-term settlements created a situation of insecurity among the intermediary class as well as the tenants and uncertain condition in the State. As a result, neither the State nor the peasants could get any benefit. It deteriorated the land revenue condition. Neither permanent settlement nor temporary settlement could give relief to the peasants.

There was a series of short-term revenue settlements introduced by the Britishers in Odisha between 1804 and 1837. The first settlement under British rule was concluded in the year 1804-05 followed by Triennial Settlement from 1805 to 1808. Second one year settlement was also conducted in 1808-1809. The Settlement of 1808 produced a revenue of ₹ 14,38,982 including Khurda and permanently settled estates of Garjat States. The arbitrary increase in land revenues were not at all related to any detailed assessment of total rent. Unlike, under Mahratta administration, British revenue administration tested bitter experience in Odisha. In the year 1817, the great Paika Rebellion broke out in Khurda. It awakened the British Government to a positive stand and their outlook towards the landed proprietors as well as the peasantry. Government realized that there was something wrong intrinsically in their revenue policy. Agriculture suffered from neglect of cultivation so as to escape revenue assessment during this period.

Actual Settlement in Odisha was started in the year 1887 and ended in 1945 by the Order of the then Governor General and certain rules and procedures for settlement was adopted. The procedures that were adopted from beginning to the end has been described by Mr. S.L. Maddox, the then Settlement Officer, in his book 'Final Report on the Survey and Settlement of the Province of Odisha, Volume I.' The next settlement was taken up in the 1890 covering the whole temporarily-settled area of Odisha including the petty revenue-free estates, as well as Killas Darpan, Madhupur and Aul, the Ekhrajat and Khandaiti mahals and it was concluded in 1900.

All this has been described by Maddox in his "Final Report on the Survey and Settlement of the Province of Odisha (Temporarily-Settled Area), 1890-1900, Volume II", published in 1920. It was commonly known as Maddox Report or the Provincial Settlement of Odisha. [11] In his report Mr.

Maddox has given a detailed account of the early revenue history and the British Settlement in Odisha before 1837 in Chapter I and the history of Revenue and Land Tenure Systems prevailed from 1844 to 1898 in Chapter III of Part III of the report. This Provincial Settlement was then followed by the Revision Settlement of Odisha (1922-1932) widely known as Dalziel Settlement. [12]

Land Settlement and Tenure System During British Rule

For the assessment and collection of revenue, three kinds of land settlements were made, such as: zamindari, mahalwari and raiyatwari. The zamindari system prevailed in Coastal Odisha comprising Cuttack, Puri and Balasore districts and in south Odisha comprising parts of Ganjam and Koraput districts. In Odisha, the zamindari system was of two types, viz. permanent and temporary. The greater part of British Odisha, especially larger tract of North Odisha, was under temporary settlement and a few states were under permanent settlement. Raiyatwari system was introduced in Ganjam district covering the taluks of Chhatrapur, Berhampur and Ghumsar. Mahalwari system, peculiar to the Central Province, had prevailed in Sadar and Bargarh sub-divisions of Sambalpur district having originally formed a part of the Central Province. The three kinds of land settlements are discussed in detail below.

When the British conquered Odisha, they found that the land revenue was collected by various land revenue agents whose names were found in the Marhatta accounts as zamindar, talukdars, mukuddams, sarbarakars, padhans, etc., some of whom represented large tracks of land and the others, single village plots of land. After establishing the rule in the State they took steps to legally vest the property right of land with these revenue collecting agents. Irrespective of individual history of rights and origin, Regulation XII of 1804 treated them as whole body of revenue agents under the common description of zamindar.

All such persons (under whatever designations they had)

discharged this function and subsequently became landlords under the British system, and this was the origin of the zamindars of Cuttack, Puri and Balasore districts. [13] Those persons were recognized as 'malika-i-zamin' (proprietors of soil) and were allowed to enter into engagement directly with the government of East India Company for the payment of revenue of their respective estates. They were the persons of certain classes of permanent and privileged tenure-holders of land whose position approximated to that of the proprietors of estates. [14]

The classes and origins of the persons of different tenure holders of land, admitted to settlement of Odisha in 1804 by the British described under different names of common revenue collecting officials were zamindars, pradhans, makadams/mukudamas/kukaddams, sarbarakars, majkuris, talukdars, kharidadars, jagirdars, bazyaftidars etc.

Zamindari Tenure: The zamindars were the intermediary between the state and the actual tillers of the land. They were conferred with the right of private ownership over a vast area of land called estate. In lieu of this, they were given the responsibility of collecting the land revenue or tax from the cultivators and payment of it to the State or Government treasury. The amount of revenue payable by the zamindar for his estate was fixed permanently or for a certain number of years and accordingly, the estate was permanently and temporarily settled. In both the permanently and the temporarily settled zamindari areas, the peasants were left to the mercies of the zamindars who raised rents to an unbearable limits. [15]

However, it was during the British rule in Bengal and in parts of Odisha and in some other States of India, tha the zamindars were conferred with the right of private ownership over a vast area of land called estate and the right to inherit and transfer of the whole or a part of their estate by sale, gift or otherwise. Such property rights of the zamindars were conditional. The colonial state honoured such rights of the zamindars as long as they paid the revenue to the State. They were accorded with the right to collect rent on cultivable land from the raiyats/tenants and the right over fisheries, wastelands and forest lands of the States. The amount of revenue payable by each zamindar for his estate was fixed permanently or for a certain number of years according as the estate was permanently or temporarily settled. The Malikana or the proprietary share of the rent paid to this rentier class varied from 30 to 50 percent of the gross produce according to different localities.

Land Reform Measures on the Eve of Independence

Among the land reform measures introduced by Britishers during pre-Independence period, 'The Odisha Tenancy Act of 1913' was a landmark Act in the record of agrarian legislations for the welfare of the peasants in Odisha. It was enacted to safeguard the interest, rights and obligations of all kinds of tenants. It made complete provision for all matters relating to governance of tenancy relationship. It ensured the rights of occupancy raiyats in their land and prohibited reck-renting. The Odisha Tenancy Act was amended in 1928 in order to meet the changing situation.

The amendment was made to make consolidation of land holdings in the State. This Act provided for the desirous tenants to exchange lands to consolidate their land. The Act Land Tenure system was further amended in 1938 to provide for the free transfer of rights of the tenant without the consent of the landlord, to ensure his right on his land to plant trees, enjoy fruits, cut and utilize timber etc. It also provided for the reduction of rate of interest on arrears of money rent from 12.5 percent to 6 percent. It also provided for the further abolition of imposition of all sorts of excess rent. Another Act called 'The Odisha Land Mortgage Bank Act, 1938' was enacted during Congress Ministry to develop agriculture in Odisha and to develop agriculture by providing loans to the agriculturists etc.

Land Reforms during Post-Independence Period

As the agrarian policy of the British Government and sporadic revisions of the tenancy laws failed to keep pace with the changing time, the first and foremost task of the popular Government in 1947 was to reform the existing tenancy laws, to make the laws instruments capable of providing adequate safety and security to the tenant cultivators, to generate in them a sense of belongingness of the land they were cultivating, to provide subsistence to the family members and to bring them in direct contact with the Government machinery after the elimination of the middlemen.

The Land Revenue and Land Tenure Committee commonly known as "Naba Krushna Chaudhury Committee" submitted its report to the Government in July 1949. The Committee recommended for the abolition of zamindari system as the first phase of land reform measure. Accordingly, as a first phase of land reform step in Odisha during post-Independence period, 'The Odisha Estates (Abolition) Bill' was introduced in the legislature on 17th January, 1950 and finally 'The Odisha Estates (Abolition) Act, 1952' came into force after receiving the President's signature. The Act provided for the complete abolition of all sorts of intermediary classes like zamindars, inamdars, jagirdars, sarbarkars, thikadars, gountias, malgujars, mafidars etc. and the elimination of all kinds of intermediary interest.

This Act made the tenants overwhelmingly happy as they felt that all kinds of anomalies in the agrarian structure would disappear and they looked forward for a period of plenty and prosperity. Thereafter, the 'The Odisha Tenancy Relief Act, 1955' was enacted, which provided for many protective measures ensuring the security and safeguards of the rights and interests of the tenants. It made a number of tenancy reforms including the regulation of rent. Another landmark in the legislative measures in agrarian relation in Odisha was the enactment of 'The Odisha Land Reforms Act, 1960' for the benefit of agriculturists of the State. The significant provision of this Act was to pave ways for the consolidation of land holdings. The first settlement operation in the independent India was started in the year 1954 and all the settlement procedures were completed in 1962.

After India's Independence, land reforms were envisaged as an important instrument of change directed at removing institutional and motivational obstacles standing in the way of modernization of agriculture and the creation of a more egalitarian social structure. Those measures were made an important and integral part of the rural development programme in the early post-Independence Planning period. These measures were specifically undertaken as basic strategies in the programme for achieving a breakthrough in the custom-oriented and tradition-bound agriculture. According to the Land Reform Division of the Ministry of Rural Development, Government of India, 'the major objectives of land reforms have been the reordering of agrarian relations in order to achieve an egalitarian social structure, elimination of exploitation in land relations, realizing the age old goal of land to the tiller, enlarging the land base of the rural poor, increasing agricultural productivity and infusing an element of quality of local institution'.

The Department of Land Resources in the Ministry of Rural Development has been playing a crucial role in evolving a national consensus for initiating effective land reforms, which include: (i) abolition of zamindari system and all intermediaries since the beginning of the fifties in order to improve the economic position of the tenants; (ii) introduction of a family ceiling and redistribution of the ceiling surplus land in favour of landless households in the mid-fifties with a view to increase the proportion of actual owners; (iii) introduction of co-operative farming; and (iv) reorganization of agriculture through the scheme of consolidation of land holdings in order to prevent further fragmentation of land holdings and to increase the size of the unit of cultivation for efficient and scientific utilization of scarce land resources and to facilitate the application of modern farm technology in agriculture.

Therefore, an ideal form of land reform programme was conceived as an integrated programme of action. As pointed out by James Putzel, redistributive land reforms had played an important role in the rapid growth that South Korea, Taiwan witnessed after World War II. China's success in reducing poverty is also the result of land reforms.

Odisha has emerged as one of the most backward states in our country not only in terms of higher incidence of rural poverty but also, in terms of very poor performance of land reforms and other pro-poor reforms. In the state, the bureaucracy dominated by strong feudal influence in the initial days after the Independence and in the latter, due to an unholy alliance with new power groups in rural society (the nexus of neo-landlords-contractors-mafia and corrupt politicians), the reform measures in land seem to have been seriously defeated. Naturally, the bureaucracy never cared for any meaningful implementation of land legislations, particularly in the absence of powerful democratic movements centering militants and consistent struggle of the rural poor.

Sixty five years down the line of nation building plans and programs, a number of problems are still far from satisfactorily resolved. Condition of rural Odisha still remains under-developed and have not been tackled through integrated rural development projects and programmes. Many rural areas are characterized by declining opportunities to earn a decent living in both the agriculture and non-agricultural activities. The problem of the persistence of rural poverty and high unemployment in the State even after more than five decades of development calls for urgent measures. The agriculture sector in Odisha has witnessed greatest decline in employment due to inadequate investment on irrigation and no reforms in land. There is growing inequality between rural and urban areas and regional inequalities are glaringly visible.

There is an increasing trend of shift/migration of the rural poor to urban areas to earn a livelihood due to underdeveloped agriculture. Migration from rural areas to urban areas is increasing. Rural infrastructure still remains under-developed and deteriorated. Rural roads are not in proper condition as expected. Power and water supply systems are less reliable and communications and media infrastructure is inadequate. Schools and other rural public and cultural facilities are suffering from lack of attention.

Besides the above socio-economic scenario, there is also a precarious situation in agricultural sector. Agriculture has developed into a dualistic structure of a relatively small number of large-size farms and many millions of small farms, which constitute 84.30 percent (Agricultural Census, 2000-01) of the total holdings. There is almost a complete absence of the competitive commercial family farms that are necessary in the emerging globalized economy. Little has been done to encourage small farm operators, who are capable of creating competitive farms to produce more. The potential entrepreneurial farmers have grossly failed to invest their time, energy and money due to a very poor credit and market structure followed by least land reforms. There has been no radical reform in land since 1962 in Odisha and the so called Consolidation of Holding Act, 1972 has been poorly implemented due to lack of political will, insincerity of the implementing agencies and poor/non-co-operation of the land owners.

End Notes

1. Fry Kenber, R.E. (1969), Land Control and Social Structure in Indian History, London.
2. Mallik, R.M. (1994), Economic Structure and Farm Viability: A Study with Reference to Two Villages in Odisha, Commonwealth Publishers, New Delhi.
3. Mishra, K.C. (1990), Land Systems and Land Reforms, Himalaya Publishing House.
4. Shah, A.P. (1976), Life in Mediaeval Odisha, Chaukhamba Orientalia, Varanasi, pp. 71-96.
5. Maddox, S.L. (1920), Final Report on the Survey and Settlement of the Province of Odisha (Provincial Settlement) (1890-1900), Government Printing, Bihar and Odisha, Ranchi, Vol I.
6. Stirling, A. (1904), An Account of Odisha Proper, Bengal

Secretariat Press, Calcutta, p. 49.

7. Maddox, S.L. (1920), Final Report on the Survey and Settlement of the Province of Odisha (Temporarily- Settled Areas) (1890-1900), Vol. II, Government Printing, Bihar and Odisha.
8. Datt, Ruddar and Sundharam, K.P.M. (2008), Indian Economy, S. Chand and Company Ltd., New Delhi.
9. Naoroji, Dadabhai, Poverty and Un-British Rule in India.
10. Pradhan, Hara Prasad (1986), Process of Agrarian Transition in India, Paper presented in a Workshop organized by CESP/SSS, JNU, New Delhi, "Institutional Reforms and Agricultural Growth", *Social Scientist*, Vol. 15, No. 6, June, p. 4.
11. Maddox, S.L. (1920), Final Report on the Survey and Settlement of the Province of Odisha (Temporarily- Settled Areas) (1890-1900), Vol. II, Government Printing, Bihar and Odisha.
12. Dalziel, W.W. (1934), Final Report on the Revision Settlement of Odisha (1922-1932), Government Printing, Bihar and Odisha.
13. Report of the Administration Enquiry Committee (1958), Vol. I, p. 17.
14. Dalziel, W.W. (1934), Final Report on the Revision Settlement of Odisha (1922-1932), Government Printing, Bihar and Odisha.
15. Padhi, Subhash C. and Rani, Sobha A. (2004), Peasants and Land Reforms in Odisha: 1936-1976, R.N. Bhattacharya, Kolkata.

Bibliography

Bibliography

Books and Miscellaneous

Agarwal, S.K. (1971), *Economics of Land Consolidation in India*, S. Chand & Company Ltd., New Delhi.

Bharadwaj, Krishna (1974), *Production Conditions in Indian Agriculture: A Study Based on Farm Management Survey*, Cambridge University Press, London.

Bonner, Jeffrey P. (1987), *Land Consolidation and Economic Development in India: A Study of Two Haryana Villages*, Allied Publishers Pvt. Ltd., New Delhi.

Das, Arunima (1994), "Impact of Consolidation on Agriculture and Resource Use: A case study in Pattamundai Tehsil", Department of Economics, Utkal University.

Dash, Giridhari (1989), "Consolidation of Holdings", *The Land System and Land Reform in Orissa*, Chapter 17, pp. 305-323.

Datt, Ruddar and Sundharam, K.P.M. (2008), *Indian Economy*, S. Chand and Company Ltd., New Delhi.

Dutta, N.C. (1968), "Consolidation of Holdings", *Land Problems and Land Reforms in Assam*, S. Chand and Company Ltd., New Delhi.

Fry Kenber, R.E. (1969), *Land Control and Social Structure in Indian History*, London.

Jacoby, E.H. and Jacoby, C.F. (1971), "Land Consolidation: The Small Land Reform", *Man and Land: The Fundamental Issue in Development*, Andre Deutsch Ltd., London.

Mallik, R.M. (1994), *Economic Structure and Farm Viability: A Study with Reference to Two Villages in Orissa*, Commonwealth Publishers, New Delhi.

Mandal, B. (2004), *Land Consolidation and Agricultural Development in Orissa: A Case Study Based on Puri District*, Thesis submitted for the degree of Doctor of Philosophy in Economics to the Utkal University, Orissa.

Mishra, K.C. (1990), *Land Systems and Land Reforms*, Himalaya Publishing House, New Delhi.

Mohanty, Bimal Kinkar (1998), *Land Reforms in Orissa*, ICSSR Project in Economics; an unpublished Research Report, Ravenshaw (Autonomous) College, Cuttack, Orissa.

Naoroji, Dadabhai, *Poverty and Un-British Rule in India.*

Padhy, Subhash C. and Rani, A. Sobha (2004), *Peasants and Land Reforms in Orissa: 1936-1976,* R.N. Bhattacharya, Kolkata.

Prasad, Rama (1992), *Impact of Consolidation of Land Use,* Printewell, Jaipur, India.

Ranndhwa, M.S. (1981), *A History of Agriculture in India,* ICAR, New Delhi, Vol. XIV, Chapter 3.

Ray, P.K. (2006), *Orissa Consolidation of Holdings and Prevention of Fragmentation of Land Act and Rules*, The Law Manual, The Law House, Bhubaneswar.

Rizvi, S.M.Z., Sabzwari, M.A. and Sharif, C.M. (1965), "*Consolidation of Holdings: A Study of the Process of Consolidation of Agricultural Holdings in Selected Villages of Peshawar District*".

Sengupta, Nirmal (2004), "Fragmented Land holding, Productivity Resilience Management", *Environment and Development of Economics*, Vol. II, Part 4, August.

Shah, A.P. (1976), *Life in Mediaeval Orissa,* Chaukhamba Orientalia, Varanasi.

Sharma, S.C. (1990), "Post-Consolidation changes in the use of Land in Balarampur Pargana (Uttar Pradesh)", *Land Utilization and Management in India* (ed.) Mishra, B.N., Chugh Publications, Allahabad.

Singh, Brijpal (1993), "Consolidation of Land Holdings in Punjab: Lessions for Bihar", *Land Reforms in India: Bihar's Institutional Constraints*, Sage Publications, New Delhi.

Singh, Charan (1986), "Consolidation of Holdings", *Land Reforms in U.P. and the Kulaks,* Vikas Publishing House Pvt. Ltd., New Delhi.

Singh, Jasbir (1976), "Consolidation of Holdings, Land Tenure and Size of Operational Holdings", *An Agricultural Geography of Haryana,* Bishal Publication, Kurukshetra.

Swadhinata Sangramare Nimapada' Shaheed Smruti Sangsada, Nimapada, by Dr. Bijay Chandra Rath, Lokanath Senapti and others.

Journals

Ballabh, V. and Walker, T.S. (1992), "Land Fragmentation and Consolidation in Dry Semi-Arid Tropics of India", *Artha Vijanana*, Vol. 34, No. 4, December, pp. 271-373.

Bansil, P.C. (1959), "Consolidation of Holdings in India", *Agricultural Situation in India,* Vol. XIV, November, No. 8, pp. 855-885.

Jena, R.K., Sadangi B.N. and Swain P. (1997), "Impact of Land Consolidation in Farming", *Agricultural Situation in India,* May, Government of India, pp. 81-86.

Kaushik, R.N. (1953), "Consolidation of Holdings in India", *Agricultural Situation in India,* Vol. VIII, No. 4, July, pp. 253-254.

Mann, W.S. (1959), "Scope for Consolidation of Holdings and Soil Conservation and Its Impact on Agricultural Production", *The Indian Journal of Agricultural Economics,* Vol. XIV, No. 3, July-September, p. 66 and p. 69.

Mavlankar, N.A. (1971), "Economics of Land Consolidation in India: A Case Study Reviewed", *Artha Vijnana,* Vol. XIII, No. 4, pp. 452-456.

Padki, M.B. (1965), "Consolidation of Holdings", *Agricultural Situation in India,* Vol. XX, No. 5, pp. 305-308.

Patnaik, Utsa (1976), "Class Differentiation within Peasantry: An Approach to Analysis of Indian Agriculture", *Economic and Political Weekly,* Vol. XI, No. 39, September, p. 84.

Sen Amartya Kumar (1962), "An Aspect of Indian Agriculture", *Economic and Political Weekly,* Vol. 14, February.

Shetty, V.V. (1963), "Consolidation of Holdings in Mysore State", *Indian Journal of Agricultural Economics,* Vol. XV, April-June, 1963, No. 2, pp. 46-54.

Singh, A. (1978), "Land Consolidation Programme in Bihar", *Yojana,* Vol. XXII, No. 10, June, pp. 29-30.

Singh, Pritam (1989), "Consolidation of Holdings in Punjab", *Yojana,* Vol. 33, No. 11, June, pp. 18-21.

Sreeram, N. (1966), "A Note on Consolidation of Holdings in Uttar Pradesh: A Field Survey", *The Indian Journal of Economics,* Vol. XLVI, No. 183, April, pp. 485-487.

Thangaraj, M. (1995), "Trends in Fragmentation of Operational Holdings in India: An Exploratory Analysis", *Indian Journal of Agricultural Economics,* Vol. L, No. 2, April-June, p. 176.

Thangaraj, M. (1995), "Trends in Fragmentation of Operational Holdings in India: An Exploratory Analysis", *Indian Journal of Agricultural Economics,* Vol. L, No. 2, April-June, pp. 176-184.

Government Publications, Reports and Periodicals

Administrative Staff College of India Report, Hyderabad (2000), '*Study on Review of Performance of Schemes of Consolidation of Land Holdings and Computerization of Land Records*' submitted to the Ministry of Rural Development, Government of India, New Delhi.

Agricultural Census, India, (2000-01), *"All India Report on Number and Area of Operational Holdings"*, Agricultural Census Division, Department of Agriculture and Co-operation, Ministry of Agriculture, Government of India.

Agricultural Census, Orissa, (2000-01), *"Bulletin on Operational Holdings"*, Agricultural Census Commissioner, Board of Revenue, Orissa, Cuttack.

Annual Report (2006-2007), *"Land Reforms"*, Bharat Nirmal through Rural Development, Ministry of Rural Development, Government of India, pp. 137-257.

Annual Report (2007-08), Department of Water Resources, Government of Orissa.

Board of Revenue, Orissa (1973), *"The Orissa Consolidation Manual"*, Vols. I, II and III.

Dalziel, W.W. (1934), *"Final Report on the Revision Settlement of Orissa (1922-1932 A.D.)"*, Government Printing, Bihar and Orissa, Patna.

District Statistical Handbook, Puri (2005), Directorate of Economics and Statistics, Orissa, Bhubaneswar.

District Statistical Handbook, Subarnapur (2005), Directorate of Economics and Statistics, Orissa, Bhubaneswar.

FAO's Report, *"The Design of Land Consolidation Pilot Project in Central and Eastern Europe"*.

Government of Orissa, (2006-2007), *"Reports on State Level Conference of Deputy Director, Consolidation and Consolidation Officers"* Directorate of Consolidation, Board of Revenue, Orissa, Cuttack.

Government of Orissa, (2008), *"Statistical Abstract of Orissa"*, Directorate of Economics and Statistics, Orissa, Bhuabaneswar.

Maddox, S.L. (1920), *"Final Report on the Survey and Settlement of the Province of Orissa (Provincial Settlement) (1890-1900)"*, Government Printing, Bihar and Orissa, Ranchi, Vol. I.

Maddox, S.L. (1920), *"Final Report on the Survey and Settlement of the Province of Orissa (Temporarily- Settled Areas) (1890-*

1900)", Vol. II, Government Printing, Bihar and Orissa, Ranchi.

Minutes of State Level Conference of Deputy Directors of Consolidation (2006-2007), Directorate of Consolidation, Board of Revenue, Orissa,Cuttack.

National Commission on Agriculture,(1976), *"Report of the National Commission on Agriculture,"* Part XV, Agrarian Reforms, pp. 323-328.

Orissa Development Report (2002), Planning Commission, Government of India, New Delhi.

Planning Commission (1966), *"Implementation of Land Reforms"*, A Review by the Land Reforms Implementation Committee of the National Development Council, Government of India, New Delhi, August.

Planning, Research and Action Institute, (1961), *'Impact of Consolidation of Holdings'*, Lucknow.

Profile on Agriculture in Orissa (2006), Statistical Section, Directorate of Agriculture and Food Production, Orissa, Bhubaneswar.

Rajagopal, Vasant Gumaste; Pingle, Gautam; Bagga, R.K.; Murti, J.R. and Mathur R.R. (2000), *"Study on Review of Performance of Schemes of Consolidation of Land Holdings and Computerization of Land Records",* Administrative Staff College of India, Hyderabad.

Report of the Administration Enquiry Committee (1958), Vol. I, p. 17.

Index

Index